Beyond

Survival Stories of African Immigrant Physicians on Life, Love and the Practice of Medicine

Compiled by:
Dr. Omerine Aseh
Dr. Nina Lum
Dr. Enaka Yembe

Co-authored by:

Dr. Sirri Bonu Mochungong

Dr. Susan Mbu

Dr. Maureen Muke

Dr. Bi Akwen Tadzong-Fomundam

Dr. Shirley Ayuk-Takem, D.O

Dr. Raissa Fobi

Dr. Isabelle Mulango

Dr. Clarisse Tallah

Dr. Anita Sangong

Dr. Irene Bih Wakam

Dr. Grace A. Neba Fobi

Dr. Luegenia Ndi

Beyond Challenges: Survival Stories of African Immigrant Physicians on Life, Love and the Practice of Medicine

Copyright © 2019 by UImpact Publishing Group
All Rights Reserved

No part of this book may be used, reproduced, uploaded, stored or introduced into a retrieval system, or transmitted in any way or by any means (including electronic, mechanical, recording, or otherwise), without the prior written permission of the publisher, with the exception of brief quotations for written reviews or articles. No copying, uploading, or distribution of this book via the Internet is permissible.

The author, writers, and publisher have made every effort to include accurate information and website addresses in this work at the time of publication, and assume no responsibility for changes, omissions, inaccuracies, or errors that occur before or after publication. The publisher does not endorse or assume responsibility for the information, author, and writer websites, or third-party websites, or their content.

Published by UImpact Publishing Group

Beyond Challenges: Survival Stories of African Immigrant Physicians on Life, Love and the Practice of Medicine

ISBN: 9781692481995

Acknowledgements

To our phenomenal leaders for governing the execution of this inspirational anthology:

- Dr. Omerine Aseh for launching this project and for her dedication and initiative towards the conception of "The Ladies Breakfast Group at ACPA" where these authors first met.

- Dr. Nina Lum for her idea and vision of this book, along with her background auditing work towards its creation.

- Dr. Enaka Yembe for her direction, coaching and expertise in the production of this masterpiece.
&

- To "The Association of Cameroon Physicians in America" (ACPA), the unifying umbrella organization that brought these fifteen authors together in April of 2019.

Table of Contents

Dr. Omerine Aseh……………………………………… 5

Dr. Nina Lum……………………………………….. 25

Dr. Enaka Yembe…………………………………….. 42

Dr. Sirri Bonu Mochungong……………………….. 62

Dr. Susan Mbu……………………………………….. 80

Dr. Maureen Muke…………………………………… 97

Dr. Bi Akwen Tadzong-Fomundam …………… 108

Dr. Shirley Ayuk-Takem, D.O ……………………… 133

Dr. Raissa Fobi……………………………………….. 152

Dr. Isabelle Mulango………………………………. 170

Dr. Clarisse Tallah…………………………………. 189

Dr. Anita Sangong…………………………………. 213

Dr. Irene Bih Wakam……………………………… 232

Dr. Grace A. Neba Fobi…………………………… 247

Dr. Luegenia Ndi………………………………….... 265

Dr Omerine Aseh
Board Certified
Family Medicine Physician

In Ceaseless Pursuit of My Dream

> *Through hard work, perseverance and a faith in God, you can live your dreams.*
> *~ Ben Carson*

What does it take to achieve a dream? Is it merely the function of time and chance? Or is success solely dependent on one's natural abilities?

I am Dr. Omerine Aseh, board-certified Family Medicine physician. The physician's coat isn't the only one I wear. I'm also an immigrant, a wife, and a proud mother of 3 kings. I am an entrepreneur, an optimist, an avid gardener, a self-taught baker and a philanthropist.

Physicians are often misunderstood, although sometimes revered by society. As a Physician, I am not unaware of the fact that many times people are quick to make inaccurate assumptions about my life. Physicians are regular people who share a common passion of applying science to help others with infirmities. They also share a very strong work ethic because they deal with the fragility of human life and are called to make life-altering decisions almost daily. The road to becoming a physician is one less traveled because it is trying, grueling, and often painful. I have walked this path and lived this experience, learning along the way the undeniable power of unwavering persistence and faith in the face of adversity. There were many obstacles I had to conquer along the way, and some stand out bigger than others.

1993, Bamenda, Cameroon

It was late in May when everyone with eager anticipation awaited the year's first sprinkle to lick up the scorching heat of the past months. The dry season in that part of the world could be so unapologetically brutal that one gladly welcomed the shelter of any kind of car to hide from its venom. I was so cozy in the passenger seat of my father's car, windows rolled down, face soothed by the blowing breeze as we sped down the tarred roads. I should have been basking in this small comfort, but I wasn't. I was clutching my report card, head bowed, chest heaving, tears rolling down in an unbroken stream as my dad stole puzzled glances my way while asking yet again, what was wrong. I finally caught my breath to say, "Daddy, I failed Form 3. How will I become a doctor?" Just saying the words reaffirmed the realty to me and I collapsed in uncontrollable sobs.

"Calm down, we will talk later," he said as he patted my hand and redirected his concentration back to driving. That was my Daddy for you, a man of tranquil demeanor and very few words. But how could I be calm when I when was weighed down with so much shame and embarrassment? Me, of the prestigious family name; the offspring of highly esteemed educators; scholarly success ought to be a given for me. Yet, here I was coming back home with a bad report card. My friends would laugh at me! My neighbors would mock me! Let the ground just swallow me already; I couldn't bear the shame. And I wailed more, louder this time; complete with characteristic noisy blowing of the nose. That was Omerine for you - a little emotional with a flair for the dramatic.

> *Faith; the substance of things hoped for; the evidence of things not seen.*
> *~ Hebrews 11:1*

All our potential is within us. Like the bamboo seed, even if we don't see any progress for long periods of time, it is still there and must be nurtured. Sometimes, the Lord allows a delay to teach us a lesson.

As we continued our journey home that fateful day, I would repeatedly steal fearful glances at my father as he drove on wondering why he wouldn't still raise his voice at me this one time. At least yell at "ma fille" for disappointing him. "Ma fille" was what my dad affectionately called me you know, meaning "my daughter" in French. His bearing exuded strength, so tall was he, with gentle eyes that always held a special sparkle for us - my mother his queen and my siblings. My mother often referred to him as the sun and we, the planets rotating around him. He was solemnly revered by the rest of society for his sharp wit, spitting out wisdom with charm in his radio-personality-quality baritone as he held court to an enraptured audience. But most of all, he was a simple man who delighted in the simple pleasures of life - enjoying a lazy afternoon on the porch to crack a joke or two with a passerby; delighting his children with stories about the "good old days"; getting his hands dirty as he lost himself in the beauty of nature in his garden; reading yet another book while occasionally taking a sip from his cup of coffee... Oh how I loathed myself and mourned the loss of his approval.

> *Everyone Needs a Cheerleader.*
> *Be your child's cheerleader!*

"Parents were the only ones obligated to love you; from the rest of the world, you have to earn it" - Ann Brashares.

Back in time…

For as long as I can remember I struggled academically. I was oriented in a very rigorous and competitive system; one which subjected students in every classroom to a numerical ranking style. What is worse, the practice in most schools was to publicly announce top and bottom 1-5 place ranked students so everyone knew how well you compared with your peers. I was a repeat offender in the bottom category; imagine the disgrace!

My biggest problem was my inability to focus. Both at home and at school, focusing on a task was extremely difficult. My overactive mind would wonder at the slightest opportunity, weaving tales of fictitious characters. In retrospect; maybe that is a craft I should have nurtured. Who knows, I may have been an award-winning fictional writer today, organizing book signings and making featured appearances on Oprah. There I go again. I just told you about my inability to focus right?

Not only was I a remedial student; I was socially awkward and chubbier than most of my peers. I was a victim of constant bullying and continually teased without mercy. School was pure torture and by age ten, the schoolyard had already convinced me I wasn't good for anything.

The Power of Words	The soothing tongue is a tree of life, but a perverse tongue crushes the spirit (Proverbs 15: 4)

The scathing words of my peers stripped me of all confidence, putting instead in its place anxiousness and constant worry. This would follow me well into adulthood and it took quite some doing for me to break off the powerful hold they had of me.

My mother ran me through the gamut of strategies that were supposed to improve academic performance - holiday classes, scolding, "pep" talks - anything that would help her daughter, become a high achiever, or an average one at worst. Funny thing is I was very curious and naturally inquisitive; I asked many questions and read voraciously to seek answers. But when it came down to formal assessments, I was terrible, hence my abysmal grades.

Anxiousness, worry and self-blame are all peas in a pod. As I worried, I also blamed myself for things I had little or no control over. When my once bright brother gave up medical school after a diagnosis of schizophrenia in 1992, I blamed myself. Maybe I hadn't been a better friend when he needed one. Or maybe the embarrassment from his sister's constant failure had driven the poor guy to the hell of mental disorder. All unfounded theories, but that was my self-inflicted guilt.

> *Everything in life is created twice- in your mind and then in reality.*
> *~ Robin Sharma*

The mind is your most powerful possession; a place where destinies are made or crushed. Positive thoughts are worth nurturing to succeed in life. Write down a vision, meditate on it day and night, speak it until it manifests into reality.

The educational system is very unforgiving, I must tell you. Make less than the required cumulative grade point average and you were forced to repeat that class all over, no excuses allowed, no mitigation considered.

Form 3 (equivalent of 7th grade in the American school system) was a pivotal level; it was the class wherein a student had to prove the level of his or her academic preparedness for the rigor of Form 4 and 5 whose curriculum prepared students to take the secondary school exit exam- GCE. I attended a prestigious boarding school, Our Lady of Lourdes College (aka Lourdes). When you think of Lourdes, envision a quasi-Ivy League school in the US. Everyday life was strongly hinged on status earned either via economic viability, social skills, or scholastic achievement. Ours was also a culture strongly founded on the greater African culture which thrived on excellence; with no place for mediocrity and no mercy for failure.

Matriculating as a Form 4 student automatically conferred influence and respect. You could finally earn the much-esteemed title of "sister". I had spent 9 terms dreaming of the day I would debut my majestic walk in the refectory halls feigning ignorance of the hushed whispers of the junior students showing off to their friends: "that's Sister Omerine". But alas, that is all it would be - a dream. Instead of respect, I would face mockery. Instead, of 'Sister Omerine", I will be "Omerine, the failure".

Life lesson: Approval

"Are not two sparrows sold for a copper coin? And not one of them falls to the ground apart from your Father's will. But the very hairs of your head are all numbered. Do not fear therefore; you are of more value than many sparrows." – (Matthew 10:29-31).

Newsflash: Not everyone will approve of you or like you! That's right! Many will not, but if the Lord himself counted us so valuable to the point of counting our hair strands, why then depend on others to determine your self-worth?

1993, Bambili, Cameroon

The 3-month holiday following my failing Form 3 was the most trying I would ever spend. It was supposed to be a time of respite and relaxation. O the joy of sleeping through the wee hours of the morning without the annoying sound of a bell interrupting your sweet slumber; the pleasure of not being subject to icy cold showers on an already stinking cold morning; nor mandatory endless daily church activities - morning mass, Angelus, rosary recital, evening devotion- whew! It should have been a time for giggling with friends, rough playing with my brothers, enjoying the company of my father and his indulgence over my "Daddy buy me this, or that"; and learning new culinary and crafting skills under the strict eye of my mother.

But I wouldn't be doing this as I suffered long bouts of indescribable shame and despair. I was shut-in, only leaving the confines of my room to eat. I began burning the hair off my arm in desperate hope of some relief. It's hard to admit, but I had the urge to cut my skin. I wanted to hurt myself, punish myself for my incompetence, for failing myself and my family. The sadness was an overwhelming abyss.

My mum's faith in me however, was unwavering. She hired a highly recommended tutor for private lessons much to my dismay. I had taken holiday classes during every single long holiday for the last three years and saw absolutely no improvement. But while the previous classes had been with other students, this time it would be one-on-one and came at a very steep price. It was costing my parents a fortune and the pressure to become better skyrocketed. Lord, help me!

My classes were scheduled to take place in my little rocky hometown of Bambili; a town of under 5,000 where the afternoon heat was blistering, sticking to the skin like an adhesive over a cut. Typically, evenings came with a mesmerizing coolness as the tip of the sun slipped below the hills, stretching in layered curves along the horizon. I would leave home, five times a week, with my cousin Emmanuel as my faithful companion, marching slowly up the hill to my tutor's house. Me ever shy; Emmanuel ever loquacious as he chatted up everyone we passed on the way.

My tutor was an older gentleman with kind eyes and a warm smile. He instantly made me feel comfortable around him, and as time would go on, confident of my intellectual ability. Math was not my strongest suite but so unique was his teaching strategy that the Pythagoras' theorem would not look like some strange incomprehensible foreign language to me anymore. I couldn't believe it! He taught me invaluable study strategies and recall techniques, and after just a few weeks with Mr. Sama, I started to feel hopeful about my future for the first time in a very long time. It began to seem like I didn't have "water" in my brain.

Life lesson: Second Chances— Paradigm Shift	A paradigm shift is a fundamental change in one's approach, mindset, or underlying assumptions. My time with Mr. Sama led to a major paradigm shift, allowing me to see myself as an intelligent, capable young girl. To be successful in life; to achieve a goal or a dream, we must know it, see it, feel it—this often requires a paradigm shift.

They say time goes by fast when you are having fun. I must have been having fun learning because before I knew it, three months had gone by and it was time for me to go back to school. There were big choices to make too before the academic year started. Should I go back to my old school and repeat Form 3 or enroll in a new, but less prestigious school and continue to Form 4? Very big decisions my parents were expecting this little 14-year-old to make. On one hand, the former would have meant living in daily shame from an entire school of familiar faces. I was breaking out in sweat just thinking about that. The latter option would mean a clean slate, new faces, bye-bye anxiety. Guess what? I went back to Lourdes to repeat Form 3. Crazy, I know but I would go back and face the music. I will get my grades up and put my naysayers to shame. I knew I could do it.

> *Life lesson: Face your Fears*

What is fear? An unpleasant feeling triggered by the perception of danger, real or imagined. I have felt fear many times. Once I had to resuscitating a patient who had lost his pulse after suffering major trauma and I was determined not to allow fear to rule over me. Fear will paralyze your mind and take control of every action to take. The Bible advises us to not walk in fear.

1993, Our Lady of Lourdes College, Mankon - Cameroon

A Catholic boarding school run by missionary reverend sisters, Lourdes was extremely strict and operated with military-style precision. The worst thing was waking up at the crack of dawn to icy cold baths even in 10-degree weather. A normal day was thus: wake up at 5am, make your bed, perform assigned chore, bathe, attend mass, eat breakfast, go to assembly, attend class, lunch, siesta, prep (study time), sports, prep, more assigned chores, dinner, lights out, sleep for 7 hours, wake up and do it all over again. A girl could not catch a break! Add domineering senior students who thrived and gloated on the cruel subordination of junior students into the mix and it became pure hell.

Punishments were meted out for the slightest offence; real or imagined, and sometimes just because. It was "Omerine Yembe clear that grass," "Omerine Yembe scrub the toilet," "Omerine Yembe why are you "brodesing" (smiling in broken English). I hated Lourdes with a sickening passion! I did persist though, making a friend or two during the hellish six years. One of those friends Nkeng, till this day, is more like a sister than friend to me. Daily I would remember my parents whom I wanted to make proud; my brothers who pretended I was a nuisance but were obviously very smitten by me and Mr. Sama, the only teacher who had ever shown confidence in my scholastic ability. When I would eventually pass the GCE with flying colors, it was for them as much as it was for me. This was also one step to becoming a doctor, and many happy steps away from the boot-camp, Lourdes.

> *Life Lesson: Work Hard*
>
> If there is one thing secondary and high school taught me is that being book smart is not everything. Albert Einstein said a genius is 99% hard work and 1% talent. Failing one exam does not make it all over. A great clinician is the one who pays attention to details and the patient, not just one who is a great test taker.

1995, Baptist High School, Buea - Cameroon

Baptist High School (BHS) was the school I attended. It was here I would blossom like the proverbial rose and where the happiest memories of my teenage years were forged. While I had found it difficult to forge friendships in all-girls Lourdes for 6 years, formed a tight-knit group of friends in just 2 years spent in coed BHS. How ironic! We were a group of youngsters with big dreams and ambitions which would have been daunting to the reasonable man. But that was us, the "Batch of Hope" as we fondly called ourselves.

In fact, not only did I make friends, I also got a best friend for the first time in my life. She was Ntoh, a fearless, sharp-tongued, sarcastic young girl with a passion for singing in the choir. Our relationship had a rough start—I didn't get along well with sarcastic people, and Ntoh dripped sarcasm without even saying a word. Ours, it will turn out, was a case of parallel opposites whose deep connection has survived for over two decades now.

In most Cameroonian high schools, you were either a science or an art student. With ambitions to be a doctor, I was the latter, signing up for Math, Physics, Biology, and Chemistry. Physics was a nightmare and I failed my first exam in a place with little tolerance for failure - students' grades determined the institution's ranking among peers which affected enrollment. That was not a risk my physics teacher was willing to take and he threw me out of his class at the end of the first term. It was a repeat of my Lourdes days all over again. But this time, self-pity had no place in my life especially not when I knew the Physics credit was imperative to a career in medicine. Come next term then, I would sneak in Mr. V's class and sit inconspicuously at the back, feigning ignorance to the fact that he had warned me not to step foot ever again in his class. Unfortunately, a few minutes into class time he spotted me. Just thinking about my walk of shame that day still makes me cringe to this day. But the classroom had a window that would allow me to listen in on lectures from outside. So, with paper, pen and a keen ear, I braved the flies and cement floor heated by the blazing afternoon sun and took down notes as my classmates jotted away inside on comfortable desks and the cooling blow of the ceiling fan. In the evening, I would hound the smartest Physics student in class for supplemental instruction. Eventually, Mr. V allowed me back into his class as I excelled in GCE Advance Level Physics.

> *Life Lesson:*
> *The Power of Persistence –*
> *Refuse to Quit.*
>
> *"Climb ev'ry mountain…*
> *Follow ev'ry stream …*
> *Follow ev'ry rainbow …*
> *'Till you find your dream!"*
> *Song by Shirley Bassey*

The great American inventor Thomas Edison made 1,000 unsuccessful attempts at inventing the light bulb. One day, a reporter asked, "How did it feel to fail 1,000 times?" Edison replied, "I didn't fail 1,000 times. The light bulb was an invention with 1,000 steps." Another great example? Abraham Lincoln. Born into poverty, Lincoln faced defeat throughout his life. He lost eight elections, failed to get two businesses off the ground, and suffered a nervous breakdown. He could have quit many times, but he didn't, and he was one of the greatest presidents in American history. He was probably great not just because he persisted, but also because he learned from his mistakes. Never give up on your dreams, always look to see how you can learn from your mistakes!

1999, Houston, TX, USA

After high school, I traveled to Houston, TX for college. Welcome to the glitz and glamor of life in the USA. Lies! The America I saw was not the stuff of my innocent fantasies. There were stately buildings and palatial homes but also ghettos so dingy that my little Bambili looked like a thriving kingdom in comparison. The people were different too—some friendly, others rude and condescending and some others just plain aloof. The children were out of control and shockingly disrespectful. I would later learn that they were being nurtured to be bold and expressive. Yeah, right! Try that in Cameroon and get the whooping of a lifetime.

I enrolled at Texas Southern University (TSU); again, more shock. Universities in my part of the world were revered places of learning whose streets were filled with students all attempting to carry the somber look of studious seriousness. Who then were these fellows blasting loud music, cruising at high speed down the should-have-been-quiet streets of my new school? Smh…

I had to take a science major if I wanted to go to medical school, so I chose chemistry. Between working three jobs and studies, there was little time for socialization save for befriending all the pre-med students. Once again, hard work and determination paid off and I graduated magna cum laude. Talk about a long way for the girl who had failed and repeated one class and got kicked out of another for poor performance.

> **Life lesson: Associate with the Right People**

In life, one needs to surround oneself with like-minded people. In TSU, my circle of friends all graduated with honors. While trying to get to medical school, I made it a point to befriend people who had the same goals. We encouraged each other with our shared vision and unwavering zeal and focus. Eagles never fly in flocks. They fly at high altitudes, much higher than most birds, and if they meet another bird in the sky, it must be another eagle and together they soar. Don't let inferior characters hold you back. Be like an eagle—watch who you associate with.

It was now time to get into medical school. I applied to schools throughout the USA and received rejection letter after rejection letter. I felt I was qualified, over-qualified even! I'd completed research, had a 3.8 GPA, honors, I finished college in 2.5 years, attended summer school, my MCAT scores were average but good enough—why did these colleges not think I had what it took? With each rejection letter, I wept for the possibility of my dream being lost after all what I had endured. At the advice of my sister, I applied and was accepted into a Caribbean medical school, but I turned it down last minute. I was accepted into pharmacy school; I turned it down. They were all good options, but not the career path I was determined to pursue.
In case you wondered; yes, I received a plethora of advice from well-meaning friends and family on giving up this

crazy dream and facing reality. I ignored those as well. I had no plan B and in many quiet moments, even I would question myself. Was I crazy? Was I wasting great opportunities? Did I not know when to give up? I firmly decided the answer to these questions was a resounding NO! Self-doubt can be insidious, but I fought it with everything within me.

> *Life lesson:*
> *Have an All or*
> *Nothing Attitude*

In 1519, Captain Hernán Cortés landed in Veracruz to begin his great conquest. Born in Medellín, Spain to a family of lesser nobility, Cortés pursued adventure and riches in the New World. Cortés was one of the Spanish colonizers who began the first phase of the Spanish colonization of the Americas. Upon arriving in the New World with six hundred men, he gave the order to destroy their ships. This sent a clear message to his men: There is no turning back. Two years later, he succeeded in his conquest of the Aztec empire. Suffice to say that a dream remains a wish unless it becomes a burning desire. It must become an obsession! (Omerine Aseh, 2019).

The summer after graduation I worked as a bill collector for Capital One and a waitress for Olive Garden. What little time I had was spent taking road trips in the little red Kia I called Molly to every single medical school in Texas. My Molly witnessed many tears, desperate prayers and sometime off-key singing as I put in the miles from on medical school to the next to hold audience with deans and program directors, recount my story, and ask what it would take for a student like me to get into medical school. Much like how I took a class from a window in High School, I was now finding new ways to chase my goals even when the odds were stacked against me. Where there is a will, there is a way; they say. My will would make a way someday, I prayed.

> **Life lesson: Mindset is EVERYTHING**

Ever wondered why the lion is called the king of the jungle when it is neither the largest, fastest, nor most powerful animal in the jungle? The typical male lion weighs 350-500 lbs., while elephants weigh 5000 lbs. - 9000 Kgs. The lion believes he is a vicious killing machine while the elephant believes he is the lion's dinner. The lion eats the elephant for lunch proving that to succeed in life; a positive mindset, a can-do attitude, and unshakable faith are everything.

It was the end of another exhausting shift at Olive Garden. It was as hot as any Texas summer day; my feet were dying for a much-needed rest and my back was hunched under the pressure of too many hours spent maneuvering heaping plates and heaving glasses through a crowded room. All I wanted was a shower and my bed and here comes my cousin with a letter for me. After so many rejection letters, I had trained myself to expect the worse, but there was always that persistent ray of excitement as I wondered if this would finally be the one.

With a skill borne out of practice, I casually ripped the envelope open. ACCEPTED! My eyes popped wider as I read again to make sure I wasn't dreaming. Instinctively, I howled into the neighborhood. "I will be a doctor," I kept repeating repeatedly as if my neighbors really cared. It was such a profound moment of fulfillment for one who had faced academic struggles her entire life to be accepted into one of the most competitive specialist courses of study.

> *Life lesson:*
> *By Any Means Necessary*
> *~ Malcolm X*

Life goals are imperative. Have a dream and by any means necessary, pursue it until it manifests.

2003, Galveston, TX

Medical school was no breeze but when fear or self-doubt wanted to creep in, I only had to remember where I was coming from to persist till the end. The medical school certificate hangs on my wall today as a daily reminder that dreams come true, but only to those who have the boldness to keep striving and trying when negative voices and situations try to deter. It took a lot of sweat, guts and determination to get me to this place and it is taking a lot of these to keep me successful here.

Present Day, Houston, TX

> *Life lesson:*
> *Set High Goals*

My aunt, Professor Mcmoli of blessed memory, was a great proponent of Norna: "Shoot for the moon. Even if you miss, you'll land among the stars." To be successful at anything, one must have the wisdom of an owl, the gentleness of a lamb, the heart of a lion, and, most of all, the humility to be led by the Lord. We are what we repeatedly do. Excellence, then, is not an act, but a habit. Aim for excellence. (Aristotle)

My life is a testament to the fact that the only thing constant in life is change. What was an obstacle could very well become a stepping stone. Today's failure definitely does not discredit tomorrow's success. So, to all those with F grades, the introverts, the obese, the bullied, those with an Attention Deficit Disorder, those who loathe themselves and feel inadequate, those who have been ridiculed and told they will never amount to anything, those who believe they are failures—I have a prescription for you. **Dare to Dream, Dare to believe, Dare to Overcome …. like me. I am a woman who overcame her challenges through ceaseless pursuit of her dream.**

"*Trust in the LORD with all thine heart; and lean not unto thine own understanding. [6] In all thy ways acknowledge him and he shall direct thy paths".*

~ Proverbs 3:5- 6 (KJV).

ACKNOWLEDGEMENT

Dedicated to all my children
Abraham Jordan, Antoine, Asher and my three faceless angels that I never had a chance to behold.
I love you more than my own life.

Dr. Omerine Aseh

Dr Omerine Aseh MD is a Board-Certified Family Medicine physician currently practicing emergency medicine in Gonzales, TX. As a result of her 8 years in medical practice, she touched the lives of over 20,000 patients and their families. She is passionate about connecting women by encouraging them to dare to tell their stories and be vulnerable.

Born and raised in Cameroon, Dr. Aseh migrated to the United States at nineteen. After two short years, she earned her Bachelor of Science degree (magna cum laude) in Chemistry/Premed from Texas Southern University in 2002 and subsequently earned her medical degree from the University of Texas Medical Branch at Galveston, TX in 2007. She completed two years of residency in general surgery at the Atlanta Medical Center, GA and another two years of family practice residency at the McLennan Family Medicine Program in Waco, TX, in 2009 and 2011 respectively.

She has a special interest in women's health and physician wellness. Dr. Aseh is a passionate philanthropist and contributes to several non-profit organizations that support educational and economic initiatives for children and women in Cameroon. She is also a self-taught baker, certified cake decorator and an ardent gardener.

Dr. Aseh is the project initiator, team co-leader and co-author of the captivating tell-all book-Beyond Challenges, which recounts the challenges experienced by African immigrant women, pertaining to life, love and the practice of medicine in the United States. Dr. Aseh is married and a mother of 3 boys.

Dr. Nina Lum

Board Certified
Family Medicine Physician

From Rejection to Resilience

There was the faint chime of a church organ on the radio, the distant hum of a church hymn, loud chatter, melodious laughter and the opening to a sermon- just the usual rhythm that signified life on a wintry Sunday morning in small town America. I faintly registered all these as I sat frozen in the passenger side of my truck nestling an untouched and now cold cup of coffee, staring into eyes grown colder than the weather outside.

"I don't think I can do this anymore, Nina", he had said without missing a blink. Straight faced he sat. His piercing blue eyes, which once twinkled with affection, were now devoid of all emotions. His curly hair, once tapered in a quaff, now stoically held down by gel as if daring me not to touch. He was clean-shaven, all traces of his designer stubble gone. The undeniable strength of his jawline with its occasional twitch; the only sign of emotion I would perceive from the man I loved, as I watched him crumble my world apart.

He was tall, nicely muscled, adorned with thick unruly curls that just begged to be fluffed. His long lashes were a girl's envy, his dazzling teeth a dentist's dream and his eyes were reminiscent of tropical oceans-so blue, so deep, so warm and yet so uncertain. Boy was he fine! He was one of those men who effortlessly elicited the unconscious second stare from strangers; one you would try to cover up with an embarrassed blush or witty comeback.

He was a preschool teacher and had all holidays off. I was a final year resident in family medicine and was off work that day. We took advantage of our availability and planned our first meeting at the mall on MLK day.

This was my first time foraying into the scary world of online dating and I was apprehensive. But the stars must have been aligned in my favor because it was like a meeting of old friends reunited after a lingering separation. There was no awkwardness neither was there the sudden quiet of unfamiliarity between strangers. None. In complete cadence as a duo in the hands of a seasoned maestro, we regaled stories of our lives- from West Africa to small town America, from the boisterous classroom to the somber hospital waiting room. On and on we went; a banter here, a quip there; laughter ringing, eyes twinkling, cheeks blushing now and then- just two strangers, yet so familiar; black and white, a picturesque image of Martin Luther King's success, enjoying the American dream he fathomed.

The holiday season of 2013 into peak winter months of 2014 were pivotal in my life. My dreams were coming true; I would soon become an attending physician just like my mother. This meant I would have the liberty to get a license to practice medicine without supervision or restriction. Hence, I did not mind working a little more that Christmas. Plus, I was the chief resident elect and felt the responsibility to "pick up slack" by filling up any holes in the schedule to ensure that my interns were acclimated and learning. Thus, I worked through most of the holiday season as the typical resident would. In retrospect I was overworked and lonely when I swiped right on tinder, and it was a match.

But I digress.

A screeching car skidding in the snow brought me back into reality from my momentary bout of reminiscence. Nina, pull yourself together; hold your head high; you're a queen, queens don't cry…like a mantra, I contemplated the words of many motivational and biblical quotes I had heard over the years as I braced myself to listen in stoic silence as my heartbreaker finished his epistle.

"I have thought this through, if we are to get married someday, I don't think I can raise black kids in America today" he proceeded to justify this unexpected Sunday morning pre-church breakup.

With fortitude finessed by years of hardship and challenge, I listened, dry-mouthed, fingers cracking on my laps as I held back the tears. "How could he do this to me? Especially at this time?" I wondered.

How we got here.

It was early December and the holidays were fast approaching. That year it was my turn to work on Christmas day, so he knew I wasn't visiting family and friends in the Northeast. I had lived in the middle of Appalachia for 1.5 years at this point and was well aware of how isolating the holidays were. Here, company was a necessity for sanity; was he aware of that? Oh, the vile words I wanted to hurl at him! Scream, cry and throw a tantrum - just anything to release the pain churning within me like molten lava. Regrettably, many years of rigorous training under the watchful eyes of my mother won.

I stared at him on my driver's seat. And in that instant, it hit me. Why on earth had I allowed this man to take the wheel of my car in the first place? This was symbolic of how metaphorically with just one swipe, I had allowed a stranger from Tinder to take the wheels of my heart; the very heart being the gateway to my body, and he was now in complete control.

Control was a position I always sat in and I could feel myself losing a part of me under the heaviness of that moment. My shoulders fell back. I wasn't sure if I could breathe enough to hear the rest of his monologue. I was suffocating in the pain that crept up inside of me.

Come to think of it, wouldn't life be so much easier if we each came with a crystal ball that foretold the day each morning? You know, look into crystal ball in the morning and know to avoid a "code blue" on the medical unit at shift change. Or avoid going ahead of destiny to find a quick fix man on the internet who will dump you right before your medical training graduation. Now how cool would that be! It would have spared me the heart-wrenching pain I was experiencing; that's for sure. But because real life is not a fairy tale, nothing and no one prepared me for the shocker I would receive that day. As I woke up that morning, there was a pep to my step, a sparkle in my eyes and the enviable glow of a young woman in love as I hurriedly hopped into the shower anticipating a 60-minute drive to attend church service with my boyfriend. Oh, the things we think we do for God or was it for lust?!

I was frozen on my drive back home, in so much shock that the wail that initially wanted to embarrass me while in his presence refused to make its ugly debut now. I could not cry. Ashland and Morehead, Kentucky were separated by a smooth sailing one-hour ride. But while the early morning's excitement had made the departure seem like a twenty-minute ride in plush luxurious comfort, the gloom surrounding the return morphed it into a journey of a thousand miles. During my unintended solace, I still wasn't sure about what just happened. Ludicrous questions flitted through my mind: "who breaks up with someone on a Sunday"; "was that even a break up"; "did I just get dumped"; "I was a good catch, wasn't I"? And on and on.

Home sweet home at last, but my little house felt cold that night. Scrubbed clean of all the day's grit, I stood barefaced in front of my dresser mirror as the truth of that day's events sank in. I was Nina, a 26-year-old resident physician and I had just been dumped. I stared at my reflection and could barely recognize the person I saw. How did I let go of my sense of self this much to where I could no longer recognize who I was staring at?

It wasn't just that I was rejected, jilted and afraid of being alone. At age 18, I left my home country of Cameroon for Curacao. Unsure of what lay on the other side of the ocean I pursued but fueled by my medical goals to navigate uncharted waters. I had no idea that a love for a career in medicine would take me from the sunny skies and turquoise blue seas of the Caribbean to the cold isolating winters in a town of 6,000 people in the middle of the Appalachian Mountains of Eastern Kentucky. This was a place where I had to explain where Cameroon was and constantly seek to prove that I wasn't *very* different from everyone else. During my first year there I was alone most of the time but never lonely. So no, I wasn't afraid of being alone. It was the disappointment from my self-imposed pain - the folly of over investing my time and resources in a man that was not as invested as I was. More so, my naivety in not recognizing that from the beginning, as superficial non-rewarding physical attributes blinded me.

The next few days.

They say it never rains but pours. A few days later I was stranded on the side of a road looking at the rusty mass which made up my broken-down truck. The devil was at work in my life, or so I thought. Just what I needed, another mishap. Yet, determined as any physician worth her salt, I still made it to work just in time to begin my clinic schedule at 8:00 am. However, 15 minutes into my first patient encounter, I hurriedly left the room and dropped the brown paper chart on the desk by the clinic nursing station and ran into the closest bathroom. It was designated "for patients only" but that was too bad. I was either going to sob hysterically in the clinic hallway or cut the line in front of all the patients waiting to collect a urine sample for a rapid urine analysis.

At the brink of embarrassing myself and disappointing my next patient, I locked myself inside that bathroom and let the tears flow. I needed to do this for myself and for the next patient on the clinic schedule. For me; it was reassuring to walk in there after releasing my hurting emotions and be the champion of the day. No one needed to share my pain. My attending needed to see I was still a competent resident physician. My patients needed to see I was confident and be accepting of my person as I created their plan of care.

How it all came together.

As you would imagine, this was not my first rodeo on the bull's back being flung away with rejection. However, this time it was different. I was rejected because of FEAR. Not my fear, but the fear of another person based on something I could never change: the percent expression of melanocytes in the epidermis of my future offspring. If that was a mouthful, then bluntly speaking, the color of my skin was a major reason for our break-up. I was black and he was white! My origin had been the source of prior rejections but never so overtly.

As my racing heart attempted to stop beating at the noise of racism masquerading as logic in the arguments of the man I dated, my thoughts took me back to another trying time of rejection. It was 2004 and I had just been denied entry into the only medical school in Cameroon after months of studious preparation. It signified the end of the only career dream I had and in dejection I accepted that medical school was an impossible feat.

With this mindset, I feared my way into developing a plan B- one driven by "hear-says" since the internet was a luxury not yet easily accessible on my dirt road. As any youth in third world Africa, I had heard so many great things about America and seen too many pictures of immaculate streets and regal skyscrapers signaling that America was the promised land of our time. It was a place we revered. We marveled in awestruck wonder at those who had been fortunate enough to taste of its splendor. Their tales of its grandeur and the blessings of success they flaunted to the rest of us who were yet to see this great place were outstanding. Studying in this place became my Plan B. However, supposedly, getting admission into any school in the US was like grasping at straws and one had to pick a study discipline in a field that wasn't readily available in one's country of origin to be granted a student visa for travel. Thus, despite medicine being my primary goal, I was quickly drawn into pre-pharmacy (as that wasn't a degree major at any of the Cameroonian public universities at the time).

With no proper mentorship and only a few college handbooks I would borrow from friends to guide me, I applied to a few schools including Temple University and Massachusetts Institute of Technology. I was so excited when I received admission into Temple University's pre-pharmacy program. But my excitement was short-lived; I was denied a visa to study in the United States. And the inner voice of my subconscious added to itself: "studying in the most progressive country in the world is also impossible". To my younger self, this equated to being a failure. When would I ever get a break? At that point, I enrolled into Bachelor's degree program in Microbiology. It wasn't anything I had ever considered but I took it on with gusto and began an attempt to love and enjoy plan C.

Oh, to become a physician!

Becoming a doctor remained my lifelong dream and this brief detour was only a part of my ultimate journey to medical school. For immigrants like myself, options were very limited hence I went to the first medical school that accepted me, although it was located halfway across the world from Cameroon, on the Netherlands Antilles island of Curacao. This admission was my saving grace. I, a Cameroonian girl who had been denied admission in to the only medical school in my country, denied entry into the US as a teenager on multiple occasions, now getting the privilege of studying in the United States! It didn't matter what part of America I was getting catapulted to.

All I cared about was ultimately being able to study to become a doctor. Thus, to steer clear of all distractions and keep my eye on the price, throughout the clinical rotation years that ushered my first 2 years in the USA, I never made dating or interpersonal relationships a priority. Nothing would come in the way of my dreams. Not a man, at least. In retrospect I was working with a limited mindset that every potential mate I could meet was likely to be a liability instead of an asset. Evidently, I never planned to someday encounter holiday blues or the common loneliness familiar to millennialism during festive seasons. Mine only being amplified because I was a non-immigrant in rural America, further away from home than others around.

One might expect that by the time I successfully weathered through the rigor of medical school, I would ooze this confident strength of self-sufficiency with every breath. But the human heart doesn't work like that, no one thrived in isolation. So, during my second post graduate year (informally known as PGY-2) loneliness slowly crept in. The advantage of being a foreign resident was in the excitement of the first-year. My first-year experience was buoyed by acclimatization and cultural adaptation experienced in a large academic teaching hospital replete with all the bells and whistles of modern-day healthcare living. Try immediately being thrown into another world to complete the rural focus of my family medicine training -a tiny mountain town of less than 7,000 where seeing another familiar face was rare. Loneliness was bound to threaten even the strongest willed. Perhaps now you can understand what drove me to making that one swipe that would leave me rejected and a broken mess of misery in the bathroom of my residency clinic.

A career in medicine is unintentionally isolating but necessary to prepare for a challenging career branded by such uncertainty that the mere stroke of a clock could turn a sane day into an unholy chaos. Isolation and rejection are two situational conditions that easily invoke emotional stress in young men and women. So, instead, of caving under the self-inflicted stress that both are prone to induce, it was up to me to use my internal fortitude and change whatever losses I encountered into wins.

Again, I tell you; heartbreak is hard, even for a mentally tough doctor! Between each patient, while my peers bonded over hallway coffee to the soothing sound of clogs as another medical personnel scuttled away, I sought solace in the bathroom. It had become my new favorite place; I could cry out my eyes here unbothered, loudly blow my nose, pat my hair and retouch my lipstick, before heading out to pick up the chart in the door to see my next patient. A lady still had to look her best, you know.

In the weeks and months after the incident, I relied on a multitude of lessons on strength, which had been ingrained in me for over two decades. Learning not to show emotion is one of the first lessons in medical practice, expressing emotion that shows vulnerability is contrary to the physician's call. To do no harm, we portray ourselves as heroines even when we feel defeated inside. Likewise, as a Cameroonian woman from a lineage of strong independent, mothers – I had been schooled on the virtues of strength. Carrying oneself with strength was a supposed enviable character that like secret kitchen recipes was transferred from generation to generation losing little of its valor even after exposure to the trials of life, be it heartbreak or rejection of any kind.

Some days were harder than others and determined to be the beacon of strength I was expected to be for my patients, and for myself, I pressed on. As the snowy blanket of Kentucky's mountains slowly melted under the kiss of many sunny days, it was spring, and then it was summer and like the flitting birds chirping in the skies, my heart could once more sing. Not from the love from another, but from deep within.

The Englishman's dictionary defines resilience as the ability to return to a previous state after being stretched, but I am of a dissenting opinion. Resilience to me is the ability to not lose efficacy and functionality despite being bent out of shape. To rebuild, rebrand and regrow after trial. In many ways; the mindset we have about how we approach challenges can be redeveloped and refined through seasons of challenges. This marks the difference between the person who gets worn down by the past to the point of losing efficiency in one domain of their lives far into the future and the one who rises above these travails and soar as an eagle would.

During the lonely months when the pain of my broken heart left me a willing captive in my house, I began to read: about the relationship struggles of other women; about career challenges faced by other women in medicine and I was utterly ashamed to realize my ignorance to my own trials until other people gave it a name. Until I became familiar with the more universal challenge of being heart broken, only then did I start to introspectively analyze all the other aspects of my life where rejection had shown its ugly head.

In doing that; I identified how that first rejection letter from the only medical school in Cameroon at the time framed my subconscious mind about rejection. I felt discriminated against because of my native roots. All those years, I was convinced that I did not get accepted because I was from the marginalized group of English-speaking Cameroonians. Yes, I grew up in the French region of Cameroon and my command of the language was decent as any native-born French man or woman. While my grades would not earn me a lifetime admission, they were not dismal. So, you see why I had to pin my rejection from that medical school to extrinsic circumstances such as ethnicity and tribe; a well-known political issue at the time and something I had no control over. Definitely, losing a potential relationship again over uncontrollable circumstances opened my eyes to the similarity we experience during the acute pain of rejection.

Own your pain

But there is beauty in learning. It propels you out of naiveté and opens you to a new world of maturity. As Oprah will say, I got my first "ah-ha' moment. The first lesson I learned from my ordeal: be open with your pain. Diagnose it, learn from it, heal from it and then share the power that came from it. Nestled in the darkness of my bedroom as if the light was symbolic of a future, I was not yet ready to face, I pulled out my iPad and began swiping. And no, not on a dating app this time around, but on web browsers as I consumed books, articles, and media with a desire to learn about myself. This opened the door into a journey of self-reflection. I began to realize that rejection did not have to define me. It was not a reflection of who I am as a person. But it was up to me to dissect causes, learn about myself and create a unique path to my wholeness. I could not hide under the façade of my job, I had to deal with myself first, to heal my heart so I could be better for every other part of my life.

Talk about your pain

From the quiet comfort I found in faceless virtual comrades, I ventured with my pain to write about it, and share lesson number two in dealing with rejection for me: talk about it. The moment I purposed to crawl out of the shell I had immersed myself into, I was pleasantly surprised to find that I did not own the trademark to heartbreak and rejection. Women and men who had two or more stories of heartbreak in their time, which mostly served as springboards for greater achievements, surrounded me. Where the story didn't inspire, it served as a wicked tale of humor on a girls' night. Some of their stories I had vaguely known of but was only now able to appreciate them through my now clean lens of empathy. I was even now beginning to covet my prized spot of being a one-time heartbroken woman, a condition I had to experience because I can now help other professional women regain their sanity after heartbreak. Likewise, hiccups are a common occurrence in most professional journeys. Hardly anyone was ever lucky to chart a career path to esteemed status free of challenges along the way. So, remember you are not alone. If anything, you are fitting in with the greats.

Turn the love you gave inward

Prior to my experience, I never stopped to analyze how the patterns of subtle forms of rejection repeatedly over the course of my live have kept me shielded from my true self. Reflecting on my journey gave me an epiphany of how I had become a master of withholding compassion from myself.

Lesson number three is to turn the love you gave that person inward, and use that to help you find yourself, love yourself and move on. It is easier to believe the lie of rejection, compounded by feelings of inadequacy than it is to belief in the possibility of a fulfilling and brighter future in the horizon. Rejection is powerful and its real strength comes into potency when you choose not to rebuild yourself based on who you truly are. We are quick to blame ourselves for bad outcomes. Just because someone takes their love away from you doesn't mean you're any less of who you are and any less worthy of being loved. Take that love, compassion and affection that you want to give to others and shower yourself with it. Specialize in self-compassion.

Acceptance is the opposite of rejection

Eventually, I moved on to complete residency with my sanity intact. I was stronger, wiser, a lot more confident, and excited as I began my long-awaited career as a board-certified physician. Herein lies the final lesson I learned from rejection: the pain doesn't last forever. I learned to give myself grace and compassion. To forgive myself of choices I made during vulnerable seasons of my life. I accepted my outcome and repurposed my pain. In writing it today, I am giving it new power. It will empower you and countless other men and women to rise up after defeat. Bathed in self-pity, I often wondered if the pain would ever go away, if I would ever be myself again, if things would ever work out well for me. Oh yes, they did. But a key point to note here is the time factor. Healing from rejection takes time. Give yourself time, because that is a crucial part of truly finding yourself and knowing who you are as a person. It is good to be single and left alone long enough to learn about you.

These days I am far removed from that state of intense melancholy. I am making new friends and reconnecting with the old. I'm still reading, but now also learning to hold the pen. I'm still growing in my career, and yes, still dating. Now unlike before, I can boast of the maturity that only time and experience can give; the boldness in asking the right questions, the wisdom in recognizing the red flags, the pragmatism in walking away when necessary, the confidence in accepting that I could never be for everybody, and the pride in enjoying myself in those times when loneliness cries out and I have no one to answer its call.

Time alone doesn't heal wounds; with God's help you heal yourself. I hope all my readers who are thrown into the darkness I once owned, will one-day smile because, I do now.

ACKNOWLEDGEMENT

Dedicated to Peter, Victoria, Carlson & Terence whom I am tied to by blood and an unfathomable love.

Dr. Nina Lum

Dr Nina Lum is a Hospitalist and Chief Quality Officer at a community hospital in Kentucky. She is board certified in Family Medicine. Dr. Lum was born in Cameroon, Africa; but in 2012 she graduated from The University of Saint Eustatius School of Medicine in the Netherlands Antilles. She completed a residency at University of Kentucky Rural Track/St. Claire Family Medicine where she graduated as Chief Resident in 2015.

Dr. Lum is a contributing author of the bestselling medical anthology "The Chronicles of Women in White Coats". As a physician coach she blogs at www.theencouragingdoc.com where she writes and coaches international medical students & graduates (IMGs) on success blueprints for their unique pathway. She is the creator & educator of the online course-coaching platform for IMG's known as imgroadmap.com. She is a health & wellness speaker and newspaper columnist for Sentinel Echo who has been featured on WLEX & Fox 56.

Dr. Lum is also an avid medical missionary and has worked with teams in Haiti & Cameroon. She loves photography, entrepreneurship, travel, blogging and reading on self-improvement. She and is the co-leader of this book; Beyond Challenges.

Dr. Enaka Yembe
Board Certified Family Medicine Physician

Shattered Dreams

I walked out of the building trembling! I already knew it but now it began to sink in. Yes! The bitter truth of my own circumstances was staring at me dead in the face. "When you sink down to the ocean's bed and you think you've struggled to the top only to find out that your lungs fill up with water at first gasp." The pain of defeat seeped through every pore of my being. I felt an unbearable load of sadness engulf me. My heart felt heavy and it beat so fast I thought it would explode. My breathing was rapid, yet shallow. My shoulders dropped forward. I walked to my car in a daze. "Where on earth did I park?" I couldn't remember.

Then it hit me again. Another intense wave of sadness. A whelp of tears clouded my vision. Then, a huge teardrop tethered dangerously on my eyelashes and rolled down my checks when it could not hang on anymore. I had failed. Everything I had worked so hard for had imploded. As I wondered through the parking lot frantically clicking my car keys, hoping to find my huge silver Mercedes Benz SUV. I reminisced about my days as a successful entrepreneur and my heart broke. Finally, I found my car and dragged my shaky body into it. Secluded in the driver's seat I sobbed loudly with careless abandon. As hard as I cried, not even the steady stream of tears trickling down my face could wash away my pain.

The realization that life had once again dealt me a cruel hand, ushered in waves of nausea which ended up inducing pain and a complete feeling of gloom. It was comparable to the same horrible feeling a physician gets when a patient takes a turn for the worse. When every single intervention known to modern medicine fails and no matter what you do, you lose the patient. When the physiologic cascade in the human body is in an irreversible terminal pathway, no intervention can change its course. That is the same feeling I had. I had lost the pride of my hands, the product of my sweat, my baby for the past eight months…my medical practice, my urgent care center.

Even as I cried, there was a flurry of questions running through my mind. Had I arrogantly taken on more than I could chew? Had I been hasty in my feasibility research? Had I relied on an unrealistic business plan? Could it be possible that the 16-hour days I spent working on the creation of this clinic were not enough for actually budding a practice? Or perhaps, the regulatory pressures facing most of my colleges had also squeezed me out of my business? I had no answers to the recurring questions, which did nothing but try to sell the lie that I was a failure. That was not who I was!

Well who am I? I am Enaka Marie Yembe. A Board-Certified Family medicine physician in practice for 14 years. I am named royalty of my tribe in remote Cameroon, with the title, Ma Yaah of Mbot. A am also a two - time divorcee, a single mother of two adult girls; a passionate entrepreneur, a John Maxwell certified coach, speaker and mentor, a philanthropist, a bold, beautiful, successful and tough survivor of multiple failures big and small. Not a very bad resume for a small-town immigrant girl from Africa, right? But you know, sometimes in moments of despair, summoning the courage to dwell on positive thoughts is the hardest thing to do.

And so as I continued to wail loudly in my SUV that day, the sense of loss was intense, the weight of frustration so overpowering that the tissue box was not full enough to dry the river of tears. I sat there sobbing. My mind went back to the roller coaster, which had been my life for the past few months. First, a broken marriage that did not quite make it to its two-year mark. Great! Like after the crash of my first marriage years ago, I was ready for yet another life-upsetting breakup. Then managing a crazy work commute: a 345 mile, six-hour drive out of state, and a long drive back after a 48 to 60-hour work shift in the emergency room. Who does that? I did. For 18 months. All while juggling life as a parent, a wife, a supportive big sister and a reliable daughter, roles which were sometimes as tasking as they were rewarding. And now this!

Life really does have a wicked sense of humor. You spend many years toiling for something and just when you are about to take a breath of relief thinking you finally made it, another avalanche of problems hit your way. That was I, all right.

You see, from about age four or five, I knew I was going to become a medical doctor. Everyone around me confirmed this. I was too empathetic, caring, responsible and sharp-witted to be destined for any other career path. And so a physician aspirant was born. Many "A grades" in the sciences through middle school, high School and a Bachelor degree in biochemistry prepared me for entrance into medical school in Monrovia, Liberia in Africa.

I had barely started medical school when ceaseless gunfire became a frequent sound beyond the walls of my tiny dorm room and crouching underneath the bed in fear became the daily norm. It was the time of the Charles Taylor led insurgence against Samuel Doe's military government. Suddenly, the tranquil country of Liberia became a deadly war zone. I was barely 21 years old, literally stranded in a foreign land in turmoil. Escape was my only option so I fled to the comforting and peaceful bliss of my parents' home in Cameroon before I became a casualty of war.

Back in Cameroon, I started searching endlessly for opportunities to continue my dream of becoming a doctor. It was another year of worrisome waiting until an opportunity opened up in Italy to pursue my medical dream. The language of instruction was Italian. My proficiency level was very basic (if that!). Suffice to say that making it through this medical program was likely going to be an ordeal with my language shortfall. Nevertheless, hopeful and determined as always, I bid my tearful family goodbye and was off to this unknown land with nothing but my passion leading me on.

In Italy, the teeth- shattering cold was what first got me. The girl who wore sweaters in the 70-degree Fahrenheit Cameroonian rainy season weather had to survive the Italian winters. In my mind, this was a clear prescription for death. But I didn't die. And what about juggling complex fulltime medical school studies in a foreign language while also working part time for food, shelter and amenities? Recipe for failure, no doubt! But, I passed, I graduated, and I completed my residency even when health complications tried to hold me back.

You can clearly see that I am therefore no stranger to challenges. Moreover, I had never let challenges hold me back. However, the loss of my medical practice was in a class all by itself. This time around I was not only crippled mentally and emotionally, but financially as well. Big time! Thinking of the financial mess I'd likely be dealing with right up to retirement was so terrifying I found myself reaching for my Bible instead of succumbing to more tears. I definitely needed God at this time. I reached into my purse for the small Gideon's bible I always carry around. I flipped it open and went straight to my favorite words:

The Lord is my shepherd;
I shall not want.
2 He makes me to lie down in green pastures;
He leads me beside the still waters.
3 He restores my soul;
He leads me in the paths of righteousness
For His name's sake.
4 Yea, though I walk through the valley of the shadow of death,
I will fear no evil;
For You are with me;
Your rod and Your staff, they comfort me.
You prepare a table before me in the presence of my enemies;
You anoint my head with oil;
My cup runs over.
Surely goodness and mercy shall follow me
All the days of my life;
And I will dwell in the house of the Lord
Forever (Psalm 23, NKJV)

As I mediated on this scripture, I was plunged back into reminiscence….

It was the first year into my residency training when I made the bold decision to go into private practice. All those insane residency hours gave me much more than the invaluable clinical experience. I also learned about the bureaucracy and regulatory bottlenecks that for physicians in institutionalized healthcare systems, could sometimes adversely affect their delivery of quality patient care.

What really was my trigger to go into private practice? Perhaps, it was an encounter I had with a paramedic. This man refused to transport an elderly patient with a condition that could quickly progress into airway compromise because her insurance may not pay for the transportation. Really? I was livid and at the same time floored by the lack of empathy shown by a medical professional in such dire circumstances when compassion ought to have been the watchword. Yet, I get it; he was only doing his job. Were these the kinds of decisions I would have to make my entire career? Cumbersome rules and regulations were making the practice of medicine anything but seamless and driving many private practices out of business. I decided, I'd rather deal with that looming fear than maneuver corporate bureaucracy. So, at the first opportunity, I took the risk to venture out on my own.

My first medical practice thrived, and I couldn't be prouder of myself. For nine years I was the successful Louisiana CEO, the likes of which are Wharton or Stanford trained. I was the successful doctor, taking care of my patients as most doctors only dream of doing. It was amazing, it was rewarding, and it was perfect!

Then, love came and boss lady cleared her desk for a new life about three hundred and fifty miles away in bubbling Dallas, Texas. Career wise, I thought it was only going to be a change of address anyway. Much as I had done in Louisiana for the past 9 years, I was going to operate an urgent care center in Dallas, TX, I thought. After all, I had done it in 2006, why would it be any different now. Ha ha, the arrogance of confidence. My challenges taught me a few lessons.

Lesson #1:
Do not re-invent the wheel. If it's working, keep doing it – the same way. If it worked, repeat the same process.

Well, that is not what I did in Dallas. I reinvented the wheel completely without putting much analysis into it. BIG MISTAKE. I relied fully on the advice of others forgetting the fact that I was an expert in my own league and that I had about 8 years of experience in tackling the complexities of starting and growing a medical practice. How did my determination override my good judgment? Overzealous? A little cocky or overly confident? I took a huge bite and started off big instead of taking small bites feeling my way around and growing from there.

And now, as I sat there in my SUV and prayed these words, "Lord, I give You total control over my situation. Handle it and direct me because I can't." I dried my tears and reminded myself that tears and anxiety were never prescribed problem solvers. Much like a sick person needing a doctor, I had to seek professional help in order to salvage my situation and clean up the mess I had made of my finances.

Lesson #2:
Back to the basics: Goal setting.

What is my why? If your reason for doing anything is strong enough, it will fuel your determination to overcome all the obstacles you will face as you work towards accomplishing your goal. For several years, I kept a list of my top 5 goals in my wallet. For about three years, I made a habit of pulling out this note card and looking at it. The note card had withstood the test of time but it was still there. It read "God, Happiness, Health, Family, Charity." As always, I refer to the scriptures: *"The counsel of the Lord stands forever, the plans of His heart to all generations."* (Psalm 33:11 NKJV).

Indeed, one must learn to get clarity of purpose by placing oneself under the Lord's direct authority. To do this successfully, one must seek The Lord, ask him into our hearts, and He will speak His desires for us into our hearts so long as we are open to listen. My "why" has always been my children, my family then others, in that order. To serve a greater purpose than my singular needs has always been a thing that fuels my engines. I am a proponent of the Chinese proverb, which says "*If you want happiness for an hour, take a nap. If you want happiness for a day, go fishing. If you want happiness for a year, inherit a fortune. If you want happiness for a lifetime, help somebody.* Likewise, "*it is in giving that we receive*" — Saint Francis of Assisi.

So as you spend time trying to understand what your true purpose in life is, remember that service to others is what brings true happiness and meaning to your existence on this earth. Reminding myself of my true calling in life (to serve others), has kept my inner soul grounded. As I reflected on my why, a sense of peace resuscitated itself in the wave of my adversity and I began to gather myself.

Lesson #3:
The balancing act.

Success in business is about keeping a balance between financial projections, realistic financial goals and a nice financial buffer. Almost everyone agrees that something has changed for the worse in our current healthcare system. The criteria that insurance companies use for reimbursement of doctors' services not only interferes with patient care, but also interferes with the treatment a patient can or may receive. Some may disagree, but it seems that the payment system now seems to be driving medical decision-making. Value-based reimbursement and a bunch of metric driven outcomes that are supposed to align payment with value and quality are simply metric driven outcomes that say nothing about the true quality of care. So many insurance systems seem to me neither reasonable effective, or fair when it comes to their payment systems. In addition, access to care is limited by high deductible insurance plans. These variables have had a major impact on startup medical practices.

But that doesn't completely exonerate me. The devil is in the details and I know that. I should've paid more attention to the financial details. I should've done what I did with my first practice in Louisiana. Back then I partnered with an accountant who gave good advice on what was financially reasonable. I should've done the same in Dallas, but I didn't. Now, I am stuck in a conundrum!

Lesson #4:
Pay heed to storm warnings.

See this thing called intuition? Nature gave it to us for a reason; pay attention to it. I remember being caught up in a beastly storm on my drive to the gym one evening. It was like a dark quiet roar. I looked up saw this horrible dark grey cloud with many dimensions fast approaching. It was the face of the beast of the storm. Yet it was fascinating. I took a quick picture with my cell phone, made a U-turn and attempted to escape it by speeding home. Of course, within minutes this powerful storm caught up with me. Terrifying blasts of thunderclaps and blinding darts of lightening shooting crisscross in front of me. The wind howled loudly, causing objects long forgotten on the now desolate highway to fly off and make contact with my shaking SUV. As lightning flashed in the sky, the thunder echoed in striking harmony. Strangely, I remained calm.

"*Take things always by their smooth handle*"- Thomas Jefferson. As always in my times of extreme trials, I fall back unto The Lord's doctrine as spelt out in the Bible "*And suddenly a great tempest arose on the sea, so that the boat was covered with the waves. But He was asleep.*" (Matthew

8:24 NKJV). Wondering if God can keep you calm and at peace once you turn yourself and all your troubles over to Him? Read this verse. Here was Jesus in peaceful slumber in the middle of the storm while his disciples were in full panic mode and desperately trying to wake him up. He felt no danger and showed his disciples that peace may reign upon you even in the mist of extreme challenges once you place yourself in the hands of God.

Why then did I find myself caught in a storm that day? As I analyzed this, I realized that I did not pay heed to the storm warnings I had received on my phone all day long. They equally came in on the radio and I had ignored them as well. Not smart. Likewise, when your business starts to crumble, pay attention to every single storm warning. Change direction early so that you don't get caught in the middle of a storm and yes even when you get caught up in the storm, do not be afraid to make a U-turn and brave your way out of it. You know why? Because there is always a calm after the storm.

Lesson #5:
The Tribe matters.

The Tribe is your family and friends; your loved ones. Your relationship with them matters as much as your thirst for professional conquests. The hustle and bustle of professional life and business can cause you to push quality time aside for all of your other responsibilities. Interaction with family members and time together is nurturing and important for the emotional well-being and development of your children and all other relationships that you have. Unfortunately, during the two years I spent trying to set-up a new practice in Dallas, I fell into the trap of being away from my family for several days in a row.

I remember the year I graduated from residency was the same year I went through my first divorce. I had to make child support and alimony payments so I worked. And worked. And worked. Sometimes, when I got off my endless shifts, the guilt would set in. I missed my babies fiercely, but work was keeping me away from them. Could they even understand that mummy loved them more than they could ever know? That she was away so much because she had to, not because she wanted to? They were only 5 and 7; I didn't know how much they could understand.

So I bought gifts. To assuage my guilt and make up as best as I could. Once I returned home after not seeing my girls for 48 hours. With guilt tearing at my heartstrings, I stopped and purchased automatic riding trucks to surprise them. Really fancy ones too, complete with cute little helmets to match. I couldn't wait to see their excitement when they saw their gifts. As soon as I pulled into the driveway, out came my little jewels with happy squeals loud enough to disturb the familiar quiet of our neighborhood. With matched enthusiasm I offered them their fancy gifts. Ta da! Eyes wide open, mouth grinning and jaws hurting from the broad smile plastered on my face. Silence… They barely glanced at the toys as they stayed glued to my legs. "No we don't want those mommy, we want you", one of them finally whispered. And with those innocent words, my heart broke once again. If only you knew baby, if only you knew…My daughters never climbed into the vehicles and never even noticed when I returned them to the store.

In all we do, never ever forget to program time with family. One good thing I learnt is to build family time into your schedule especially if you have a busy schedule. *"Behold, how good and how pleasant it is for brethren to dwell together in unity"*! (Psalm 133:1 NKJV).

Lesson #6:
Protect your most valuable asset – you.

The online dictionary defines self-preservation as *"the protection of oneself from harm or death, especially regarded as a basic instinct in human beings and animals"*. During the two years it took for me to work towards the startup of the new medical practice in Dallas, I basically sacrificed my whole self. My mind, my body, my time and all my energies were so immersed in taking care of others, the new start up business, paying rent and employees for the practice as well as for my home out of my pocket that I basically forgot to preserve myself.

Every week I drove 350 miles or so to Louisiana, worked for about 48 to 60 hours, barely slept and turned around and drove straight back to Dallas. Upon my return home I immersed myself once more in taking care of everyone else. I was determined to do whatever it took to make sure that everyone else was taken care of. I gave and gave so much over and over. Yet, no one but my mother stopped to check in to see exactly how he or she could help lift any burden off my shoulders. Mum selflessly sacrificed her time to move in with my family and I so that she could help me. Eventually, I became bitter about allowing myself to be used by all around me so much. It was no longer even about how much people around me, or the crumbling practice demanded of me. It became about what was expected of me even when I didn't feel like giving anymore of myself.

In retrospect, I should have given up a yes for a no more often; I should have taken care of me too. As I looked back over the events of the past 2 years, I promised myself to protect the most valuable asset that I possess which is me! I asked myself what I could do better going forward and again I went to the bible: *"But may the God of all grace, who called us to His eternal glory by Christ Jesus, after you have suffered a while, perfect, establish, strengthen, and settle you."* (1 Peter 5:10, NKJV).

Lesson #7:
Loss is inevitable

There is a common saying that no parent should have to bury his or her child. It is out of order. Children should be the ones to bury their parents, but that doesn't always happen. Ask any business owner and they would agree that a new business is like a child. You have this infant in your arms and then the love you had known takes a whole new meaning. Parents spend a lot of time protecting, enjoying and worrying about their children, no matter how old they are. The younger the child is, the sharper and the more acute is the parent's protective instinct. This is the same instinct one must develop and grow with any entrepreneurial endeavor. Watch over it as closely as you would a child.

The events of December 1st, 2016 are forever engraved in my mind. I was driving to my new clinic in Texas with my mother. Word had reached us that my older brother who was already very ill back home in Cameroon had taken a turn for the worse. Yet stubborn as a mule, this man refused to go to the hospital. So, my mother and I called him. His voice, clearly audible, came through on speakerphone and was surprisingly strong. "Ah you guys worry too much" he admonished. "It's getting late. I will go to the hospital tomorrow." There was no convincing him otherwise, so we let it go; tomorrow for him was only 7 more hours away anyway. But less than 4 hours later, another call came in. My older brother didn't get to see tomorrow. He was dead.

I was overwhelmed by a great sense of grief and despair-mourning the death of a sibling, beating up myself. I wondered if I, the physician sister had done enough for him as a patient even if was all the way from the other side of the ocean. I struggled to console and comfort my mother who was going through a parent's worst nightmare. For her it was a repeat pain; this would be the second son she would be burying. My heart ached for her.

I was by her side as we travelled to Cameroon to bury her son, my brother. The strength I witnessed my mother exude throughout this ordeal changed me forever. We were in church for the funeral service. It was my mother's turn to thank everyone. She stood up. My heart beat faster as I thought to myself "will she be able to do it?" I sat straight up in my chair, tensed my muscles and was ready to jump to her rescue if her knees buckled. But they didn't. My mother made it up to the pulpit. She spoke with a strong voice. Eloquently for about 5 minutes. Then she turned to my brother's picture and nodded her head. "Thank you, my son," she said as she looked at this life-sized image of him up there by the alter. "You have done well, and I am proud of you. Go well. Go be with Jesus." I held back tears even as I beamed with pride watching her standing tall at the lectern. Then she burst into song with a clear and melodious voice:

> *Move on move on don't be frightened,*
> *The savior understands,*
> *No turning back;*
>
> *Move on move on don't be frightened,*
> *The savior understands,*
> *No turning back*

Good-bye my son. Bye bye Nging Nging. I love you." With that she was done. She walked down from the pulpit to her seat. Sat down, held her purse and looked straight ahead, waiting for the last announcements to be read. Wow! My jaw almost dropped. I was blown away by her strength and courage.

In that instant, I learned that one must face tragedy when it strikes. And it would strike whether via the death of a loved one, sickness, a broken relationship, or a business failure. You name it, it will happen. With business, the longer you have been in it, the more familiar you become with failure. But the heartbeat, the core of the business that is you, your goal and your purpose must never expire. The bible says:

"Turn yourself to me, and have mercy on me, for I am desolate and afflicted."(Psalm 25:16 NKJV). The sentiment expressed here shows that perilous or desolate times are inevitable in life. However, rest assured that even in perilous times, the Lord does not turn away himself or hides his face from us.

Lesson # 8:
Expect Loneliness as an Entrepreneur

Loneliness is a thing to anticipate when you go into business for yourself. Whether or not you are a successful businessperson, you will get some degree of loneliness.

Growing up as a child I was very lonely. I was obese, made fun of and bullied because of my weight. I felt very self-conscious and ugly from an early age. I wasn't like the other pretty girls my age who preened and danced around in preppy dresses. Moreover, I was the only girl in my family until age 12 and my brothers weren't always eager to play with me. Thus, I was caught between being a tomboy and a girly girl.

Like most children from middle class homes in Cameroon, my parents made huge financial sacrifices to send me off to boarding school at the age of ten. Mine was comparable to an Ivy League institution in the US and beyond a culture of academic excellence was a social culture heavily premised on pedigree and physical looks. I was the daughter of middle-class civil servants - cancel pedigree. Tallest and heaviest student in my class- definitely - cancel physical looks. Without the pedigree or physical looks to match left me with minimal social interactions and consequently a very timid and self-conscious young lady. In fact, I was a social misfit if you went by the standards of my society at the time.

I was a recluse. First three years of boarding school, I was very unhappy and had no friends. Most of my time was spent in huge crowds, but I was always alone. And I was always thinking- of ways to make friends, to be more sociable, to stop being unhappy. Just 10 years old and I was such a big thinker. To ward the unhappy feelings away, I would sit alone and think of the old folk tales and songs my grandmother taught me. Those always made me giggle. I also thought a lot about how I wanted to become a doctor and in my imaginary mind I "played doctor". Sweet fiction! Finally, a world in which I was noticed for something other than being the subject of cruel jokes. I could hardly wait for the holidays, which were short-lived, and I had to return to my hellhole of boarding school and loneliness. The rigid schedule imposed by the no-nonsense Catholic Reverend Sisters. I hated boarding school at that time but today, I appreciate the lifelong lessons of hard work, resilience and discipline.

As a businessperson, you will experience a different kind of loneliness. I was fortunate to have grown up accustomed to loneliness. Therefore, I lived a lonely life even though surrounded by people. You must learn to embrace loneliness when you go into business. Use this time to create, learn, structure, grow, and manage your business. Loneliness is also a good time to seek God. Therefore, do not be afraid of loneliness. Even the Bible tells to *"be strong and of good courage, do not fear nor be afraid of them; for the Lord your God, He is the One who goes with you. He will not leave you nor forsake you."* (Deuteronomy 31:6 NKJV)

Final words...

While success masks our mistakes, failure gives us the opportunity to reflect, and improve. When I lost my practice, my dreams were shattered but the lessons learnt were priceless. I tell you, experiencing challenges will definitely arm you with the tools you need to gain strength of purpose and of character. Would I start a medical practice again someday? You bet I would. Would I make the same mistakes I made? You are darn right I probably will not. Would I make other mistakes? Most likely. However, I am not giving up. Like my mother, I have squared my shoulders after my grief and I am ready to dare again. Believe it and you will.

ACKNOWLEDGEMENT

Dedicated my best friend Leonie Mpafe Samuto. I don't have enough words to thank you for being the legs that always carry me along when mine become 'too broken' to support me.

Dr. Enaka Yembe

Dr. Enaka Yembe is Board Certified Family Medicine Physician practicing general medicine and emergency medicine in Louisiana. As a result of her 14 years in medical practice, she has touched the lives of **over** 30,000 patients and their families. She has also inspired and motivated hundreds of individuals nationally and internationally into doing exactly what's necessary to achieve their goals and their dreams.

Dr. Yembe was born in Cameroon, Africa. Completed a Bachelor (Honors) Degree in Biochemistry in Nigeria and medical school in The University of Milan, Italy. She did an internship in Transitional Medicine in Howard University Hospital in Washington DC and then her Family Medicine Residency training at LSU Conway Hospital in Monroe, Louisiana and was nominated Resident of the Year in 2005.

Dr. Yembe is a passionate philanthropist who founded the Omer Yembe Foundation in 2015. She brought healthcare to about 4,000 poor people in Cameroon, Africa and awarded scholarships that enabled about 100 orphaned children to go to school.

She is an avid entrepreneur who went from a zero income to 7 figures in 18 months. She is a John Maxwell certified Speaker, Coach and Mentor. Dr. Yembe was the 2019 Oschner LSUHCS Monroe Commencement Speaker. She is author of the Amazon number 1 best seller Grow to SUCCESS; Co-author of two bestsellers, Success

Chronicles and 20 Beautiful women, Africa Edition. She is also a co-leader ad co-author of this book; Beyond Challenges. She has been seen on Fox 14 TV and NBC TV.

Dr. Yembe recently launched her online e-course coined The EVOLVE Method. This is a 6 step method designed using all the weight loss tips she learnt over a 9-year period, and which helped her loose 70 pounds in 2 years.

She is a mother of two girls, a marathoner, loves personal development, travelling, dancing, cooking and taking care of her goats.

Dr. Sirri Bonu Mochungong, MD

Educational Commission for Foreign Medical Graduates Certified Physician

My Doubt, My Fuel

"Our doubts are traitors, and make us lose the good we oft might win, by fearing to attempt." ~ William Shakespeare

Like a shadow, it mirrors my every step; an intricate part of me which I struggle daily to overcome. It has been part of me for as long as I can remember. Yet every day I hold on to the consolation that tomorrow will be better; it has to be. Perhaps, I will be successful when I get into a residency. Maybe, I will be successful when I move out of my mom's home. I am sure I will be successful once I am independently taking care of all my daughter's needs. Like a religious mantra, I repeat these to myself every day in a bid to assuage the fears that seek to terrorize my very being. IT IS MY DOUBT. Unexpectedly, it creeps into me, and then I am not sure what to do next; I question and hold myself back.

From the moment we are able to reason as humans, we start dreaming of the things we would like to do or accomplish in life. Maybe it is to set many a stage alive for millions of adoring music fans; shape inquisitive young minds within the walls of a classroom; or manage complex family affairs as a diligent homemaker behind the white picket fence. For me, the sterile walls of the hospital had always been my silent call. As a child, I dreamed of the time when I would perfect that brisk walk, white coat trailing, stethoscope dangling, barking out orders to my team as we rushed on like superheroes on another lifesaving mission. Yes, I know; I watched too much TV…But here I was two decades later into life, letting fear and doubt hold me back from attaining that dream, minus all the theatrics of course.
Then in early 2010, a phone call from my mother spurred me into decisive action. A friend's son had recently gained admission into medical school in the Caribbean, she said.

Well, lucky him. Or, was it just sheer luck? Had I applied to medical school yet? No. The fear of rejection was extremely paralyzing even before I tried. However, in no time after that phone call from my mother, my application was on its way. Who would have imagined it? Two weeks later, an interview offer came! That was quick! And it made me wonder why I had allowed doubt to hold me back for so long. Nostalgia pushed to the side, I scoured the internet for interview practice questions. I was not about to jinx this wonderful opportunity. And what would you know; I performed so well that three weeks later, my acceptance letter was in. That was even quicker!

In a flurry of excitement and trepidation, I was propelled into action. First, quit my job. Fearful? Check. The next four years were going to be hard without a steady and comfortable source of income. But I would survive. Next, find someone to take over my mortgage. Happy? Check. Who wanted to be unemployed and in heavy debt at the same time? Finally, find some to take care of my daughter. Tearful? Check, check! That was the hardest decision to make. This would be the first time I'd be away from her. Would she understand, resent me, or even be able to cope without me? She was only three years old; just a baby being forced to grow up beyond her years. As I made plans to change my residence in the upcoming weeks, I toiled with this thought.

April came in before I knew it, and I had to be in the Caribbean April 10 to start classes on April 12. It was only a few days away and still I had not come to grips with the reality of leaving my baby behind; nor had I quite found the right words to explain to her confused little self that mummy was going way for a while, but not going away forever. I couldn't quite explain to her why I was going. I mean I could, and I did but all I saw was her looking at me and asking,

"Why?" As a parent, there's nothing more stabbing than the question of why from your child. Why are you leaving me? Why are you going away? Where are you going to? No matter how many times I answer this question, she was searching for only one response: "It's ok. Mommy is not going anywhere". This was the answer she would wait for in vain. I couldn't tell her that and with silent sobs from me and loud wails from her, mother and daughter were separated.

But Kiara wouldn't be alone. My village stepped in to help with her care and they were there for her all through my stay in medical school. Her Godmother, grandmother (my mom), her bevy of aunties (friends and sorority sisters) all made sure that Kiara never lacked a sense of normalcy and I could worry less about her and more about school. But, I tell you, I was the typical mom and worry about my child I did. I laugh now in recollection and wonder how these women so patiently put up with my incessant calls and now silly sounding questions.

Me: What did Kiara eat today?

Them: Plantains and fish.

Me: Did you remove the bones before feeding her?

Them: Yes [probably sighing in exasperation like "who doesn't know to debone before feeding a three-year-old fish?"]

Or

Me: [on a cold winter morning] *How is Kiara dressed this morning?*

Them: Blue tank top, white shorts, red...

Me: [screeching at the thought of hypothermia] *In this weather? Why? She…*

Them: [laughing at my dramatic frenzy] *Ha ah Sirri, calm down. I was just kidding. How else would I dress a four-year-old in wintry weather, if not warm?*

Me: [now laughing at my stupidity because this is my mother

I am talking to. She'd raised more children in her day than I could count. Surely, she knew a thing or two about weather appropriate gear. Yes, I know; I was extra! Very extra. But what can I say? First-time mom away from her child syndrome, I guess.

Anyway, back to medical school chronicles…The start of my journey also marked the continuation of my journey. Like now, when life throws you into a perilous situation; not being able to see a clear future, no way to turn around, and yet having to find the strength and courage to stay the course. But I'm jumping ahead of myself.

There are many parts of my journey where I can only give credence to divine intervention. First, it was so easy for me get into medical school; a feat which for some takes several years and several attempts. Then, I walk into medical school and boom, it is an immediate hit with my roommates. Just like that! Within me, I was deeply convinced that God wanted me on this journey.

Like every new chapter in life, I walked into medical school with a thought process of "I can conquer it all." I had made some major sacrifices especially being away from my daughter so I told myself, "I'm away from my daughter so I have no distractions. I have a goal". When doubt wanted to show its ugly head, I recited my new mantra: "I will finish medical school in the four years it takes. I will pass every exam; I will match into residency and I will once again have my daughter full-time by the end of four and a half years from the time we first parted." Ever heard of the saying "if you want Jesus to laugh make a plan"? Well, I could tell you a thing or two about that. Not that planning is wrong by any means. But just that to every plan, a backup plan is imperative and potentially, a backup to the backup plan as well if you get my drift. Stay the course, know what you're searching for, know where you're going; but by every means, have a backup plan.

I had barely acclimated to the hectic monotony of medical school when the first storm hit. January 2011. On that fateful January day, my day had started like any other but ended unlike any other. In the morning, I nervously walked in to take a Biochemistry test I had stayed up all night preparing for. I walked out of the exam to receive the kind of news I had never spent a minute preparing for. My brother was dead. Hidden in my much too quiet room, I tried to evoke memories of him but all I got was a blur. Not that I'd forgotten what my brother looked like; no. You never quite forget one whom you spent most of your childhood days with. But for us, distance was our nemesis. He lived in Cameroon and I in the United States, so we had not seen each other for years.

So yes, we were no Siamese twins, but we were siblings all the same and news of his death hurt me more than I could ever imagine. For six hours, I sat alone in room, remembering the long conversations we used to have; some only quite recently. In silent meditation, I realized I'd give everything for just one of those now. As the tears finally started trickling down my face, I let go and for an hour I cried my heart out. Then, I was done. I would only continue again after my exams were over. For now, it was back to good ole medical school.

Life continued. But before I could take the veil of mourning off, it was news of my daughter needing major surgery. Hard as the thought of a child's surgery can be on any parent, it was even harder for me because I could not be physically there for her. Instead I was miles away, only available via daily video calls to let her know mommy still cared. Oh, and to make it worse? My mother tells me my daughter's father hadn't bothered to drop in make a single call since her ordeal. Not once before to wish her well, nor once after to ask how the procedure went. And here I was thinking at least she had one parent by her side. True, you can't force a horse to drink water, but you can at least lead it to the stream, right? Therefore, while I couldn't force him to call or go see his daughter, I could remind him how parental love and concern was important for her, especially during this time of convalescence. So, I called him and urged him to do the right thing by his child.

It was September 2011, time for another challenge. This time, I failed my Pharmacology exam, and shortly after, I failed my Pathology I exam. To say I was stressed out would be an understatement. Barely one year into Medical School and I was already boasting failure in two critical exams.

Prior to matriculation, I had been advised by older students, faculty and counselors how my school, St. Mathews operated. You only get to retake a class once before you are sent packing. Oh, and the USMLE step 1, 2 and CK exams? Do not try to fail any of these if you didn't want to find yourself saddled with a mountain of debts and no place for residency after wasting four years of your life. The well-meaning advice was not meant to sow a seed of fear into the minds of the young medical students about their

ability to succeed. Instead, it was meant to drive and motivate us to do our best and to study harder than we ever studied. It was a seed to instill in us a drive for perfection by which we would forever be judged as physicians. Armed with this knowledge, I forayed into medical school knowing that failure was not a luxury I could afford to twiddle with.
I just couldn't understand how I failed any of these exams. I mean, I'd done my part as a student; diligently attending lectures, taking notes and studying into the wee hours of the morning. Stairway to success, right? Wrong. You could still study and fail if you were studying the wrong way for the task ahead- first lesson medical school taught me. Well, who knew there were different and unique ways to study for an exam in each course? I didn't.

With failure come two choices: 1) learn from it and move on to correct identified mistakes next time or, 2) wallow in pity and refuse to learn from it. And many times, it is easy to defer to the latter as it takes less will power to seek that easy route than the much harder one of positive determination. When I failed, the ugly seed of doubt was planted within me yet again as I drifted into fear and self-pity. Even more depressing for me was when I again failed Pathology my second try, despite all my best efforts.

I was at a crossroads now. Quit before I get kicked out, or try transferring to the closet school that would take me, while I still could? I wasn't sure. But my mother was able to convince me that quitting medical school altogether was not an option. My roommates had gone through the same struggle that I was facing, and they had already gone ahead to secure admission into a new school.

I conducted my research and settled on International American University. I had barely three weeks to apply, interview, get accepted, and transfer and while I scrambled to meet the seemingly impossible exploit, I decided to implore the mercy of my Dean once more. He was my Pharmacology teacher, had watched me work hard to reverse a fledging score to a stellar passing grade in one semester. He more than most knew my potential and was well placed to make an exception based on mitigating circumstances. But alas, rules were rules. They couldn't be broken, he said. Or perhaps rules could be broken for the right people at the right time, just not for everyone every time. But if rules could not be broken in your favor, then just maybe it was not meant to be.

Accepting my fate, I packed all my belongings and set off for a new island in December 2011. St. Lucia was my new home, and I fell in love with the quaint little country of expansive beaches and friendly people. However, I reminded myself I wasn't here on a tourist trip; I was here to earn a medical degree. Before that, I had to conquer my fearful giant: Pathology. Having already failed it twice, this was my last chance before I bade goodbye to all dreams of a medical career. I was given the option to take both pathology I & II which would spare me the need to spend an extra semester on the island. I grabbed the opportunity with both hands.

While tackling Pathology I & II, I took on the role as mentor for Year 1 students. My repertoire of study materials proved helpful to those behind me. I was a natural fit for the role and felt with each passing day that this indeed was where God wanted me to be. Passing both Pathology exams here only helped to increase this conviction. You didn't miss that, did you? Yes child, I finally passed the much-dreaded Pathology exams and was well on my way back to the United States, home sweet home at last.

In retrospect, life in the Islands was fun; much like a well-paid touristic experience on a student's budget. I experienced the carnival without paying an arm and a leg in high season tickets, relaxed with my books on beaches that millions spent thousands of dollars to only experience for five days in a year. I made new friends, created a new family and grew into my own skin. Or perhaps out of it, if you consider the fact that I was able to lose 60lbs without even trying hard. It was quite ironic too; for most of my life, I had been morbidly obese and tried to no avail to shed off some of the excess weight. In America I was always very conscious of my bigger size but in the Islands no one cared. The beaches were a galore of people of every body size wearing any and everything. And there were no surprised stares from strangers and hardly any fear of seeing one's face in a viral video in some wanna-be blogger's edition of fashion faux pas.

Being in the Caribbean felt like being in Cameroon once again especially for a girl who had grown up in a Cameroonian idyllic beach city. For the first time in my adult life, I got to love the skin I was in and shed all doubts about my body even before I started shedding the pounds off. It would seem like this was my own special weight-loss tonic as the absence of body-consciousness seemed to have acted like a weight loss aphrodisiac. Really, I wouldn't be too surprised if I end up in the Caribbean when I retire. But that is still a long way ahead, and before that there is the USMLE exam to take.

It was June 2012 and I'm back in the US. I am finally reunited with my daughter, family and friends. I am greatly involved in my Cameroonian community. My social calendar is full, and life is fun. But I still have medical exams to take and I am studying on my own using all the study skills I had picked up in medical school. I felt I was on the right path, but the results of a practice test shook my resolve. I was nowhere near as ready as I thought I was. So once again, I packed my bags and set off for a self-imposed sabbatical at Highlands University in Las Vegas, New Mexico.

For one month, it was a grueling schedule: twelve-hour study in the library, ninety minutes in the gym, and thirty minutes meditation, check on my daughter and then sleep. No distractions, just rigid structure which seemed to work well for me. Exam day came and I remember thinking this was it; success was my only choice. I had gone this far and could not afford to renege now. But in the back of mind, the doubt was also slowly creeping in. What if I failed like I had done in the past? What if, what if, what if… The doubt kept growing with each passing day as decisive Wednesday crept in. It is the third Wednesday from when you take your exams; the day when you get the results that would either propel or end your medical journey.

Tuesday night I was too scared to sleep, and Wednesday morning, I was too restless to stay in bed past 7am. Yet even while awake, I was still too afraid to open my email. What if I failed? But then, what if I passed? The warring thoughts were driving me crazy and I decided to put an end to them by opening my email. Forty seconds became a lifetime. PASS! Come again? Still PASS! I wouldn't even bother to check what score I made. Did it even matter? Absolutely not! I had passed, my journey would continue and that is all that mattered.

I had finally made it to clinicals which meant a twenty-one-hour drive alone to Atlanta. But I'd gladly take three of those trips over an aborted medical career, thank you very much. So I embarked o
n the road trip to Atlanta; blasting oldies in my car and taking in the sights of Texas, Louisiana, Mississippi and Alabama along the way. Guess who also happened to be

doing clinicals in Atlanta that same time? My roommates from St. Mathews! Once again, the "snugthugs" were reunited- that is what we called ourselves from the days we lived and supported each other in Snug Harbor through trying times in medical school.

One thing clinicals did was to quell any lingering doubts and reaffirm that this is the profession for me. Not because it was revered by society, not because the entry way for me had been seamless; and not because my mother wanted it for me. No. The daily interactions with patients brought me such intense joy and fulfillment that I just knew that this is what I wanted to do for the rest of my life.

After taking all the necessary rotations, I signed up for step 2 CS. This was supposed to be the easiest of the three exams, still I had to take it seriously. It was based on clinicals, an area wherein I thrived. Building a rapport with my patients came easy to me. One patient said it was my warm smile and another said it was just some air of comfort I exuded. I have no idea. But whatever it was, getting patients to open up came easy for me.

But while I basked in this natural talent that would make Step 2 CK easy for me, I did not take note-taking, which wasn't my biggest strength, into consideration. Consequently I failed the exam. In came the doubt and not just any doubt. The big down, the one I had been afraid of from day one. Like in the past, I shoved 'Mr. Doubt" away although it took me another three weeks to muster the courage to register for the exam again.

On the day of the exam I met someone. Eric. He walked up to me after my first break and out of the blue asked what I thought would happen if he went down on one knee and proposed to me. Huh? Who was this clown making me pierce the quiet of the exam room with my crazed laughter? Turns out he was a friend of my family, even if he only knew me by name, and I him not at all. But his unusual introduction was just what I needed to ease my exam tension. A great friendship was formed that day, and a medical exam was aced.

On April 10, 2014, I faced yet another huddle. My father had a stroke and after going through medical school, ignorance was no longer my ally. I knew what a stroke meant, and I knew how devastating its outcome could be depending on scan results. Now, given my medical school pursuit, I was the pillar of knowledge for my family. I was also the voice of reason and source of comfort for my brothers. We relied on faith in God and science that dad would make it, but it was not to be so. On April 17, 2014, he took his last breath.

I was as devastated as any child would be over the loss of a parent; perhaps more so because I was a Daddy's girl through and through. But by now, I had become adept at burying my emotions. Mentally I knew my daddy was gone, but emotionally, I refused to deal with it. So like I'd done with the death of my brother, I mourned while buried in the familiar comfort of medical journals. As one in a trance, I made the trip home to bury my dad, and came right back to continue with study for the next board exams.

Just as I got ready to take my exams, my school decides to implement a new rule: passing the NBME with an acceptable score is now a prerequisite for taking the Step 2 CK exam. For me, earning the said acceptable NBME proved to be an uphill task. Five times I took the same exam and five times I received the same result: Fail. By now, my clinical rotations were long completed and I was back home and ready to for the Step 2 CK exam, if only I could pass the NBME. And I thought Pathology had been a pain. Ha!

These days, my mind was a battlefield between doubt and hope with the former gaining victory most days. Then there was the incessant voice of my mother urging me to "just register for the exam again one last time". If I thought her nagging at the time, I am grateful today because the sixth time for me was the charm. Finally!

I was as ready for step 2 CK as I would ever be and didn't waste time to schedule my exam. On the morning of the exam, I gave myself a pep talk: failure is not an option, you have come this far, you have to make it etc. You know, all the motivational gibberish one can fathom to suppress fear and doubt. Exam taken and the anxious wait for another decisive Wednesday begins. Only this time, the message was negative. FAIL! And for the first time in a rocky journey of 4 turbulent years, I cried my heart out. This was the end of the road as I could see it. All the hard decisions, life changes and disruptions. Not to talk of the financial toll, the self-doubt from every failed exam, and the demoralization over having to take a single exam 6 good times…In fact, just everything. And now this!

A few weeks later however, I was on my way to Orlando, Florida, and not for a tour of Disney like most visitors. I was there for a six-week course; another sabbatical for the purpose of study. At the end of my stay, I felt I was ready to attempt the Step 2 CK exam again and I was right. I broke into my happy dance as this Wednesday's email showed the only word that would finally bring this long globetrotting journey to a happy end - PASS. Finally, Dr. Sirri Bonu.

This journey taught me many things; perhaps most importantly about the crippling power of doubt left unfettered. Doubt clouds your mind to success and makes failure your only focus. Had I not consciously tried to suppress doubt with hope when I failed, I would never have made it to the end. Even after passing the dreaded Step 2 CK exam, my woes were far from over. You see, I did not match into a residency program. Eric stepped in to help me get an interview at his program, and I had a second interview in Staten Island. I was so convinced after this that I would match into that program at least but that would not be the case.

Many days I was riddled with doubt. Do I graduate? Do I deserve to graduate? What am I going to do when everyone is talking about where they matched at graduation? But I fought those lingering thoughts with positive ones as soon as they emerged. I took time to celebrate my graduation because I deserved it. I worked very hard for my degree and no one can ever take that away from me. So come graduation, I was as happy as every one of my peers; beaming with pride, strutting the stage in full dark green fringed academic regalia to collect my diploma, and smiling for so many pictures my face hurt. As my dear friend, Comfort, succinctly put it, "not everyone can go to medical school. So, celebrate it because not everyone finishes medical school". True words for one who had almost not finished medical school. I could so relate.

In August 2018, I am blessed with another opportunity via divine intervention. I am introduced to Dr. Yembe who without thought or hesitation takes me under her wing and allows me to do an observership in her program. I have been able to see another side of medicine; rural medicine and under her tutelage, I have learned better interview skills.
Match season 2019 rolls in and I am excited. I have one interview, and I'm convinced this is it. But it was not. Life

goes on and I spend my days preparing for step 3 in a bid to better my application.

What makes today different from yesterday you may ask? Well, today I see my doubts, I acknowledge my doubts, I own my doubts, and I'm determined to move past my doubts. Every day I ask, every day I answer, and every day I remind myself that to be without doubt is not human. It's simply not possible. Even the disciples, great men of faith, doubted Jesus. He walked on water yet they doubted. They tried and they sunk till he brought them back up. I am no better. I will fall time and time again, but each time, I will rise to share my story so that those who have gone through my similar struggles will know that they're not alone. Someone has been there. Someone is there and someone has come out on the other side. I am fortunate to know many who have come out on the other side. Because I unashamedly share my story, I am certain that they will be inspired to share their experiences also. Together, we will continue this cycle of sharing to reassure that someone out there with doubts that, you are not alone and you too can overcome.

With that I remain hopeful; it is just not my time yet. But my time will come and so will yours too. In the meantime, use your doubt as the fuel to your destination.

ACKNOWLEDGEMENT

Dedication: God for village, Comfort for core, Kiara for grounding, Family for support.

Dr. Sirri Bonu Mochungong, MD

Dr. Sirri Bonu Mochungong MD is an Educational Commission for Foreign Medical Graduates Certified Physician applying for the 2020 Residency Match. Dr. Bonu migrated to the United States at thirteen to Lansing, Michigan. She then relocated to Indiana where she received dual degrees; Bachelor of Science in Biology and Bachelor of Arts in Criminal Justice from Indiana University Bloomington; followed by a Masters of Business Administration from the University of Phoenix and a secondary one from Davenport University. Dr. Bonu attended medical school on the beautiful island of St. Lucia at International American University where she graduated December 2017.

Dr. Bonu is a member of Zeta Phi Beta Sorority, Inc an organization that allows her to spend time giving back to the community through volunteer activities at her church, local food drives, and mentorship opportunities for the kids of CAM-NM. She enjoys everything health and fitness, and has taken this passion and shared with others as a Fitness coach and a Live Core De Force certified instructor. She can also be found lighting up the Zumba dance floor and cliff jumping. Dr. Bonu utilizes her business degree as co-owner of Si-Sisters.

Dr. Bonu adds author to her portfolio as a co-author of the must read motivational exposing book - *Beyond Challenges,* which follows 15 immigrant African women through doubt, failure, broken hearts to emerge resilient, faithful, determined and successful in the field of Medicine in America.

Dr. Bonu enjoys spending time with her family, and is driven by the resilient and hardworking nature of her national award winning competitive twelve year old daughter ice skater.

Dr. Susan Mbu
Internal Medicine Physician

The Silent Fight

I opened my eyes and squinted at the sunshine streaming in through my bedroom window. Then, I squinted again as I sensed a throbbing sensation. I tried to stretch but grimaced and hissed a breath through clenched teeth. My legs felt weird; my chest like a pile of lead. I could feel my fists tighten, not knowing whether to continue silently screaming as I suffocated with each breath I took. I was just waking up from a long night's sleep, yet my strength left me, even as I attempted to stand. I ran my fingers through my hair, to calm the silent tussle within. I bent forward, pressing my palms to my bed and suddenly, my throat held back something between a sob and a shout. Something must be wrong.

The chirping of the birds alerted me yet again to the break of dawn as the vibrant rays of the sun filtered into the still of my little room. It was now 6am and I was supposed to be starting my daily routine: 2-mile run, then catch the bus for a full day of classes, labs, and crunch study at Essex County Community (ECC) College in Newark, NJ. It was a fully packed schedule for an ambitious seventeen-year-old with very big dreams. But for the first time, my well-coordinated schedule was interrupted with no prior warning. As I laid in bed unable to move under the weight of this strange sensation, I realized something was definitely wrong.

With the stubborn determination, which has characterized my very existence to this day, I clamped my teeth to suppress the wave of pain and dragged myself out of bed. There began my ordeal. As the days turned to months, it felt like my body was held together by a heavy brass magnet. Yet I trudged on, even as I was reduced to a wreathing mass on one too many floors, blinded by the onslaught of never-ending pain. There were days when my body felt numb with pain, like fingers of ice gone numb by wintry wind gusts in icy chaos. There were days when it would have been a blessing not to feel at all. Days when the need to curl up and cry was greater than the need to breathe. Days when I wished I could take the pain away.

Oh, the things we take for granted! Little tasks such as writing, and chewing became much-dreaded; every step I took was carefully calculated and my daily two-mile runs became a vague memory of glorious days past. The only diurnal occurrences I experienced were achy, swelling joints and stiffness which seemed never-ending. Much to my chagrin, my interminable supply of over-the-counter medications only seemed to exacerbate rather than abate my suffering.

I was a long-way from home, in a foreign country, oceans apart from the love and nurture of family and those that raised me, with a minimum wage paying part-time job. I earned just enough to splurge on $10 after all my bills were paid every month. Owning health insurance was definitely a luxury and not even an option. Well, what would you know? Finding a doctor who would see an uninsured patient was much harder than selling ice to Eskimos. I had almost exhausted all the phonebook entries when I finally lucked out and found a general practitioner who agreed to see me despite my circumstances.

She was compassionate, a migrant from Ghana who was moved by the seething torrent of tears I shed over my predicament. I explained to her that I had no guardian or parent to represent me and make sense of the medical jargon she spat out. After a series of probing questions and a medical exam, she gently asked me with a solemn look:

"have you ever heard of rheumatoid arthritis?" No. I replied. "It is a crippling autoimmune disease that affects the joints", she explained as I stared at her incredulously. Apparently, I had all the signs and symptoms for it. The only word that kept ringing in my head was "crippling" and my next question was hinged on fear unlike I'd ever experienced in my young life: "Am I going to be on a wheelchair"? With a voice laced with compassion for her terrified young patient, she answered in the affirmative. There was no cure yet for the disease so, there was a possibility that I could progress to that state should the disease become aggressive. The universe seemed to conspire against me and everything good was about to implode.

The silence was nothing but a shield for my sheer disbelief. I breathed in real slow. I couldn't dare blow up. Pinch me! Somebody wake me. This is a bad dream gone too long. Ha Susan! I wasn't even old enough to get an unrestricted driver's license, barely old enough to vote, still bound by curfew laws in most counties and someone was telling me I may never walk? Like ever again? I was an enthusiastic young girl: running was my passion, participating in a 5k run on my to-do list and throwing balls on the court my ideal mode of socialization. I was excited to wear my mini-skirts, eager to go dancing with friends, and looking forward to strutting in my high heels occasionally too; what young girl didn't? But alas! What a mirage it all was. The reality was strong enough to burst open the floodgate of tears I'd been trying to suppress. As the first tear dropped, not even the steady stream trickling down my face could heal my hurt as I mourned the death of dreams shattered too soon.

I was to continue taking non-steroidal anti-inflammatory drugs such as naproxen readily available over the counter. However, I would need to see a Rheumatologist too. Very funny. How is that even possible with no health insurance? Therefore, unable to refer me to one, I slumped my shoulders in utter dejection and prepared to leave her office as the tears trickled anew. I vigorously tried to wipe my tears as I left her office wondering what kind of future awaited me as a disabled girl.

Just the night before, I was longing for my eighteenth birthday. Not because I wanted a big celebration, although that would have been nice; but because I might get a full-time job that offered insurance benefits. But that was still months and months away which meant that in the meantime, the scourging pain, stiffness, and swelling would continue to be an unwelcomed daily companion. However, I worried more about the goals I had set for myself and what will happen if I could not take care of myself. Life offered me very limited choices.

School was on full swing; I was soon getting a degree in Biology Pre-Medicine. I had also secured a scholarship to Montclair State University to continue my bright academic journey. It should have been a very exciting time for me; burning the midnight oil all those nights was paying off. I should have been on the Internet, feeding my eyes with Montclair's stately red and white buildings scattered around the large quiet campus as I fantasized about the Red Hawk life. I should have been thinking about dorm life; would it be Bohn Hall or perhaps Blanton Hall? What about Greek life? how would it feel to be part of a sorority? Would I even have the time to join any? Decisions, decisions… Yet, I wouldn't spend the summer contemplating these like most hopeful undergraduates do. Instead, I was busy setting new goals and creating concrete plans for what would happen should I be unable to fend for myself in the near or distant future; decisions most people make close to their golden age. I was making them now. I was only seventeen.

Out of school for the summer, I traded my textbooks for educative reads on Rheumatoid Arthritis (RA). I traded TV time for more reads on Rheumatoid Arthritis, and traded sport time for even more reads on Rheumatoid Arthritis. Rheumatoid Arthritis seemed to have consumed my entire young life. I soon turned eighteen and immediately got another job as a Nurse Aid progressing soon after to be a support counselor for mentally disabled patients. Working was an ordeal as the nonstop pain and stiffness proved to be a great barrier to the easy performance of my duties. Co-workers complained about me being slow; our eyes would lock when they stared in curious wonder when I walked, perhaps wondering why one so young should walk so slow. Yet because I looked overall well, it was hard to convince them that I was just not lazy, but truly sick.

What were my goals before RA, you may ask? After arriving the United Stated at barely fifteen years of age, I thought the sky was my limit. I had heard of the endless opportunities that were available in the Land of the Free with hard work. I was here to partake of the national cake, and I would not abuse this opportunity. I was of middleclass status in Cameroon; my parents were great providers and never for a day did I have to worry about earning my keep. In Cameroon, I was the sheltered princess. In the US, I was the store attendant bagging groceries to bring food to the table. Welcome to America!

When I voiced my desire to become a medical doctor (MD or DO), people would laugh in derision. Doctors here were the sons and daughters of the select elite; taking up a career in medicine was like taking up sportsmanship in Polo or Lacrosse, pedigree was the keyword. So, I wouldn't blame the people who tried to tell me to take off my rose-colored glasses or give up my lofty dream; they only meant well in their minds. Stubbornly, I held on to the dream, juggling between school and work while acculturating to a different world. Many times, in the night's stillness, I would cry in silent frustration, wondering what devil drove me to trade the comfort of the life I had in Cameroon, for this torment, but the dawn would offer renewed strength and I would push on.

I was enrolled in a community college in pursuit of my GED while simultaneously preparing for the college entrance exam in which I would eventually earn very impressive scores. I was beyond elated and rushed to register as a Biology Pre-Medicine Major. My plans were to transfer to a four-year college after two years to earn a bachelor's degree then, head to medical school right after that. I was well onto the path of becoming a physician by the age of twenty-four. Did you hear that? Twenty-four! This girl was determined and nothing would stop her.

For many, the teenage years are a time of wild exploration; it was a time to test the patience of parents, limits of society and excesses of self. It may be the only time life would ever give one the opportunity to enjoy all the vanities of youth with untamed exuberance. I did not know all these; and even if I did, I did not care to miss out on all these. I worked, studied, worked and studied again. Countless hours were spent in the library perusing the Occupational Outlook Handbook and then mapping and fine tuning my plan.

I avoided counseling; the few times I forayed into it led me to conclude it was a useless fit for me. No one was encouraging my dream, all they wanted to do was persuade me to change my planned path. I didn't need that.

I like to say I pledged Greek during my collegiate journey if only to console myself that I too had a well-rounded collegiate experience. Good grades earned me an induction into the Phi Theta Kappa Honor society. Not your regular Greek organization I know; but hey, Greek is Greek, right?

Meanwhile, I had completed a work study program and got my Nurses' Aid license but could only work part time due to my age. Funding my studies was another story. Initially I could get financial aid at ECC but that soon fizzled out in the subsequent years when I had no one to stand in as my guarantor; a mandatory requirement for a minor as myself. I would run helter-skelter knocking on every door I thought could offer relief. I found many ears to listen, some sympathetic eyes to behold a desperate seventeen-year-old lost in a foreign land, but unfortunately no eager hands to help.

So, I pursued the other avenues less easy to tread- scholarships, grants, work study, any job or work to earn a few dollars…I relied on them all. Finances were very tight, and budgeting was hard. In the comfort of my little creaky apartment, I became an astute mathematician and seasoned financier, budgeting every dollar long before the paycheck came in. A few hundred and rent was paid, thirty gone and the monthly bus pass was secured, another thirty there and my belly was filled with bread and ramen noodles from the Chinese grocery store or Dollar Store all month long; a hundred went into the tuition savings account and I still had $10.93 left to splurge. That was my life; penurious, yet very hopeful. I lucked out one day when I stumbled into a place called "Labor ready" which took anyone seeking work the same day and paid the minimum wage. I did this several times and was grateful to have some little extra cash coming in every month.

After going through all these, an ill-fated malaise was now compelling me to give it all up? No! I would beat this illness even if it was the last thing I did.

Finally, the card was there, resting inside an envelope I had just ripped open from the mailbox. I felt a sudden flare of joy. Sunshine filled my soul. My joy was palpable; a lottery winner had nothing on me. My insurance card was here! First thing- book an appointment with a Rheumatologist. With growing trepidation, I walked into his office that morning for more testing. A second opinion because we had to be sure I had been properly diagnosed. Test results showed that I had been. Next was establishing a treatment plan and off with prescriptions for methotrexate and steroids I went on my expectant way.

But if I thought I would beat rheumatoid arthritis just like that by chugging down a few pills, I was in for a very rude awakening. That first therapy offered no relief, so we switched to another one after a few months. And then another…and another yet again until we had tried nearly all the drugs on his list. Still the pain increased in leaps and bounds, this time accompanied by its evil cohorts- harrowing weight gain, unsightly rashes and elevated liver function- all unfortunate side effects of the different medications I tried. At night I was a frozen mass, turning to change my position not even an option. In the morning I was all stiff bones, running my hands under the cold water for much needed relief.

My follow up appointments were now just to routinely remove the fluid accumulation in my knee joints. Test results revealed that my inflammatory markers were elevated to such high levels that my rheumatologist feared that mine was one of the most severe cases he had ever seen in his career. He was a veteran with many years of practice under his belt.

As calmly as he could, he tried to prepare me for the possibility of a new life; it was likely I would become crippled should the symptoms remain uncontrolled. Call it faith, call it indignant disbelief, or perhaps stubborn determination but I just wasn't buying his prognosis. No sir! " I will not be crippled. I will go on remission", I calmly responded. I had read somewhere that some people go on remission after a while. He concurred; it was a possibility albeit "very unlikely and rare". Still, a possibility and that was enough for me. I left his office that day repeating my new mantra in my head "I will not be crippled, I will not be crippled".

Ah, but this funny thing called life! Desire a thing so much you could taste it and even faster it flees. I had thought getting an insurance card would mean a quick end to my problem; it wasn't. Or maybe all those medications would be the promise of much needed relief; none was. So, during one episode of agonizing pain with teeth chattering in convulsive bursts, legs mangled in torturous defeat and hands too stiff to touch, I lost it. This wasn't just crying; this was me begging-no imploring God to just have mercy on me and take my life so I could finally have peace. I had tried to be strong, but my young body was completely sapped of all its strength. My body hurt and my heart ached. The pain was too much for one person to bear. How could this be called living? I longed for death, but even death was far from me. God heard me not, or perhaps, He just had great plans for my life.

Amidst all these were some monumental firsts which I celebrated with immense delight. I started driving, a manual drive which I had to quickly trade for an automatic. Stiff hands and achy joints made driving an ordeal, but I was grateful to get to school and my variable jobs quicker. I also started looking at alternative medicine since conventional medicine gave me very little hope. I heard stories about people that suffered from conditions that were deemed incurable, living meaningful lives and even reversing the disease.

I took a trip to New York in pursuit of a doctor from the Caribbean who boasted of his past accomplishments in helping patients reverse diseases of all sort. Who knew if he was a quack boasting of medical credentials he never earned? Or maybe a doctor with a license revoked for malpractice now operating in free rein without any supervision? A desperate person asks no questions. I was desperate and naive; I asked no questions. Per his advice, I was to stop taking all the prescribed medications, replace that with homeopathic regimen, live on a daily diet of only fruits and vegetables. Say what? Again, a desperate person would do just about anything to get out of a bind. So, even if I wasn't particularly excited about this regimen, I acquiesced completely ignorant of the fact that abruptly stopping a high dose of steroids like what I had been taking was potentially life threatening. As it would turn out, taking that route almost did cost me my life and no one had to tell me to forget Dr. Wonder-of-many-accolades.

Illness took its toll on me in more ways than one. My grades suffered as much as my body did. I saw my almost perfect GPA dwindling down with every exam. The result of too many lecture hours wasted because of my inability to hold a pen, talk less of writing; and too many hours wasted battling the agony of pain. It was a tough decision to take, I finally had to listen to my body and take a semester-long sabbatical from academia. When I returned, I was forced to make an even tougher decision- trade in the medical school dream for a junior college degree. I wasn't giving up my dream altogether, however. It would only be for a while I hoped; at least until I was once again healthy enough to tackle the rigor of medical school. But still I cried for this unwelcome detour, and I cried for the uncertainty- I didn't know when or if I would ever resurrect my dream of a career in medicine.

Respiratory Therapy wasn't such a bad choice. Because I had already completed all the pre-requisites it would only take me a year to earn a degree in this major. By the age of 19, I was a gainfully employed degree holder and well into two years of living with daily acute pain. During that time, I had tried every kind of therapy there was out there: big pharma, acupuncture, acupressure, Tai Chi…, jumping back and forth like a Ping-Pong when the respite from each remedy proved to be short like all its predecessors. Don't ask me why I continued flirting with all options with their lofty promises of miraculous healing. Again, I was desperate. In my insatiable quest for healing, I stumbled upon an alternative medicine center which suggested a heavy metal detox with Chelation therapy administered intravenously. It came at back breaking cost, exacerbated because the physician visits were not covered by insurance. Hmmm, could I afford it? No. I was just a respiratory therapist. By no means was I rich. Did I try the Chelation therapy though? Absolutely yes! Pinch a penny here, save a dollar there; my college days had schooled me and turned me into a savvy 'budgetnista.'

And so the journey of no relief continued- working nights, being unable to sleep during the day, going back to work again at night all stiff, agonizingly achy, and now tired too. It was a scene from my former jobs being played all over again: the curious stares of colleagues and the not too quiet puzzled whispers about the girl not advanced in age who moved with the strength of one well into her twilight years. I was used to it by now and it didn't bother me anymore. Or perhaps a fresh start was just what I needed. I had read that warm weather had a somewhat inverse effect on pain tolerance. I dreamed of warm skies, endless summer days and fewer winter nights, and a place unlike New Jersey where a dollar could stretch very far. And with that I found myself with the few belongings I had to my name en route to North Carolina.

First call, get a job-tick. Next, find a doctor-tick; and lastly, revive my dream of a career -tick! It was six years after that first diagnosis which had thrown my world into upheaval, but that was ok. The race they say is not to the swift. Starting now was better than never starting at all. I worked weekends, spending the rest of my days in studious dedication- as much as RA would allow me to, to complete all the prerequisites for admission to take the Medical College Admissions Test (MCAT). My new rheumatologist also gave me the best news I had heard in a long, long time: there was a new medication on the market that could help halt or slow joint damage. Ah, God bless science! I was beyond excited to get my first dose of this injection but when I saw the cost, I swooned. Twenty-four whopping thousand dollars a year! Insurance coverage? Covered, but I didn't always have insurance; the premiums were much more than I could afford. Tell me, where was I going to get that kind of money from? But try I did, reverting to the frugality which had become second nature to me.

To my pleasant surprise, this little liquid miracle was well worth its price tag. Its weekly doses would be the first that ever gave me any significant relief amongst all the others I had tried. I could chew my favorite foods without the looming fear of pain; I could sleep through the night, even roll and enjoy the expanse of my queen-sized bed in peaceful slumber. I could wake up and sprint straight into the shower without first spending thirty minutes with my hands immersed under to loosen the stiffness; and could finally savor the sweet smell of nature once again as I took an hour walk around my neighborhood. Little things I had once taken for granted were simple pleasures I was now relishing and thanking God every day for.

I was now twenty-four, the year I was supposed to be graduating from medical school according to my master plan. Yet, here I was, having aced all the prerequisites for medical school but deeply worried if I should or could still attempt medical school. The naysayers had much to say to fuel my fears too: I was too old (at 24?); I needed to be thinking of getting married because it would be almost impossible for me to find a husband after medical school. Medical school was too expensive and lengthy a commitment to make. Was I strong enough to go through it? On and on they went and in a moment of weakness I almost threw in the towel and gave up on in defeat. In quiet solitude however, I would ask myself if this was "my dream" or "our dream"? The former it was so, like a stubborn mule, I took the MCAT and applied to medical school, not thinking of how I could fund it. Tomorrow would take care of itself.

Ultimately, I gained admission into medical school. The few people I told about the acceptance were pessimistic about my decision, so I celebrated in solitude; it wasn't against the law to pop a bottle of champagne by one's self.
I started medical school and it was everything I had expected to be, and then some- intense, challenging, fast, isolating, sometimes lonely, but always exciting. There were courses with straight As and others where a mere C was a welcome relief. And all this while, I continued taking my injections and enjoyed less symptoms over time. Four years later I would stand in a crowded auditorium alongside my peers, tears of joy cascading down my cheeks participating in the commencement ceremony in a trancelike state, hardly able

to believe that I was finally graduating from medical school. Yes! My prayers rose to the Heavens.

The shrill ringing of my pager roused me from my thoughts. It is a little after 6pm and I had been on my feet since 6am. I was bone-tired; surviving on a cup of coffee and a sandwich hastily heated in the cafeteria. Such is the life of a resident doctor. Some days were long, some busy, others chaotic, where your pace is only interrupted by the occasional bathroom break or a brief hasty bite. It may be a daunting for some, but for me it was the answer to many prayers made in bitter desperation all those years ago. I was finally living my dream and I would not complain.

One thing dealing with rheumatoid arthritis taught me was gratitude. Losing the ability to do simple things and being subjected to jarring pain taught me about the fragility of life. It is good practice to be thankful for everything- the good, the bad, and the ugly.

Another lesson learned from dealing with rheumatoid arthritis- just go with the flow. I was the girl with the well mapped plan: community college, then university, medical school, MD or DO by age 24. But life would give me a rude awakening, detouring me in ways so unimagined that I would have laughed in derision had one ever warned me about it before. But that is life for you; unexpected as thunderbolt. It breaks us down, but only temporarily so. And in those times, all we have to do is pick the remnants of our broken pieces and move on to create new experiences.

You may wonder if I ever was healed from the rheumatoid arthritis. The answer is a resounding no. I am still under the mercy of daily medications, relying on the coping mechanisms I had finessed over all these years. In my career life, I have had the privilege of diagnosing and treating those with the same condition as myself. When a patient breaks down under the crushing weight of this condition so painful that one wouldn't wish on an arch enemy, I have been able to hold their mangled fingers, look into their weary eyes and sincerely say "I understand" as only another comrade on a battle front can.

All those years when in agony I prayed for God to just take my life away, I would wake up wondering why He bothered to spare my life yet again. Did He have a greater plan for my life or was He just too unbothered to answer me at all? Did He truly care for me even though He allowed this horrendous ailment to plague me? Was He even listening to me at all even as I cried out to Him in grueling desperation? Perhaps, I was spared to one day be the vessel of healing to a desperate patient. Perhaps, I was spared to be a beacon of hope, a ray of sunshine, an instrument of love... Or perhaps, I was spared to tell this story. Because we would never know as we can't decipher the mind of God, I am doing all these to the best of my ability.

I am Dr. Susan Mbu, Internal medicine physician and this is my story.

Dedication
To my parents for strengthening my wings so that I can fly higher.

Dr. Susan Mbu

Dr. Mbu is an internal Medicine Physician. She was born and raised in Cameroon and came to the United States when she was fifteen years of age. She started her Career as a Nurses Aid and became a Respiratory Therapist at the age of nineteen. She earned her Respiratory Therapy degree at University of Medicine and Dentistry /Essex County College in NJ, and a Bachelor of Science in Interdisciplinary Studies and a Minor in Biology at Winston Salem State University in North Carolina. She completed medical school at Edward Via College of Osteopathic Medicine in Blacksburg Virginia in 2015 and her residency at University of Florida-Sacred Heart Hospital in Pensacola, Florida in 2018. Prior to starting medical school, she worked as a Respiratory Therapist for seven years.

Dr. Mbu is the co-author of the book Beyond Challenges, where a group of female migrant physicians express their experiences and struggles, not only in Medicine, but in life, love, and health while trying to integrate into a different culture.

Dr. Maureen Muke

Board Certified Internist and Department Chair of Medicine

The Tough March to Match.

Your vision will become clear, only when you look into your heart. Who looks outside, dreams, who looks inside, awakens."~ Carl Jung

All I could do was stare transfixed at the intrigued faces around me. Each gasp and silent moan were uttered in an attempt to quell the myriad of sentiments raging through their minds. I could feel the raw emotion, knowing they were borne out of genuine fascination and sheer astonishment. In that instant, I realized the power of a singular story.

I had the pleasure of growing up with my grandmother. Veronica Eneme was a very strong woman. She was wise beyond her years and spewed out words of wisdom with every utterance. Huddled around her feet on warm starry evenings, she'd hold me captive with enchanting tales of the past laced with African adages. *"Little by little said the thoughtful boy, moment by moment I will try,"* was my favorite. Not that it made much sense to me. Why would a carefree child in a bustling Cameroonian beach town, Limbe, be concerned about trying times when the opulence of nature: rippling serene waters, curtain silk skies and palm tree lined streets are yours to be savored with every new dawn?

I carried that carefree attitude when I set sail to the United States from obscurity in little known Cameroon. For the first time in my sixteen years, I was forced to encounter the reality of life. The first shock was seeing my mother, the Cameroonian licensed physician, juggle work and residency training all over again just so she could practice in the US. My mother did all this while raising an energetic infant and a boisterous teenager (me). Grandma was right, *"the beginning is always hard for the beginner"*.

People would be quick to say I had a very easy immigrant experience given the fact that I had a parent already striving towards attaining middle class status to pamper me. But they could not be further from the truth; my mother has never been one to serve unmerited favors on a platter. I had to earn my keep and chart my course. However, typical with any teenager, youthful exuberance came with its fair share of rebellion and wistfulness and I indulged full on. Even while I saw my mother work so hard, I compartmentalized those lessons I took from her experience, unaware of how well they would serve me in the future.

A year later, I charted off to college in Boston and college was fun! Greek activities, collegiate sports and other extracurricular activities saw me keeping late nights and missing too many classes and assignments. The ensuing effect was a massive hit to my GPA which subsequent semesters of studious dedication could not salvage. Without adequate time to seat for the MCAT and therefore no MCAT scores, attending a US medical school became a near impossibility. Faced with the reality of having almost aborted my lifelong dream of a career in medicine, I had to consider the next best alternative, thank God for good scores on my premedical courses: a Caribbean medical school.

Now, if you know anything about the medical profession in the US, you would know that within its circles, even the best Caribbean medical schools gets a side eye in a roster of medical school rankings. My disappointment faced with the grim reality of what my days of youthful lethargy and nonchalance had done to my impending medical career was palpable. But, come fall, I was among the new batch of buoyant M1's eager to earn the highly respected appellation of "Dr." While many of my peers only had to make a journey of a few miles or a journey within the United States, I was boarding an international flight to Antigua for a chance of a lifetime.

Antigua was a sight to behold and a tourist's paradise: serene cascading waterfalls, deep blue seas fringed with clean white sand, fresh tasty fruit stands at ridiculously cheap prices, rum shops, paddle boarding, night clubs that stayed open all night, and beautiful views at the campus. Still reeling from the mistakes of my undergraduate years, I disciplined myself to only partake of Antigua's beautiful distractions in small balanced doses. However, when the chance came to groove with Prince William when his ship made a pit stop on the Island, I definitely did not miss that rare opportunity. If that isn't an accomplishment in its own right, then, I don't know what is.

The jury may still be out but I consider myself a Caribbean medical school success story. To be honest, I believe the only thing easy about the Caribbean medical school was its matriculation. Other than that, it was hard, if not harder, than a US medical school. Remember those lessons from my mum and grandmother? They proved indispensable. Consequently, what effort I put in paid off tremendously. I graduated medical school! Seeing the beaming smiles on the faces of my parents was enough to transform any iota of laziness left in me into an avalanche of zeal. It was a special time for me. I had just met the love of my life, Paul; we were recently engaged, and I had a clinical rotation lined up in Baltimore while awaiting Match Day. The lines were falling in pleasant places and I was well on my way to conquer the world.

Matching for medical students is like the Holy Grail. You might be wondering what "matching" means. Match

Day is the day you find out where you will train in your desired specialty. For some, Match Day is pure joy but for others, it can be more like a bad date. Truth is, going through medical school and amassing those egregious school loans is worth zero if you do not match into and complete a residency. Even worse, failing to match during your first attempt dwindles the chances of matching subsequently to almost nil.

On Match Day, Friday March 9, 2012, I remember waking up with a spring in my step. I was ecstatic that this would be the day my journey as an internist would begin. I opened my email eagerly and read: "We are sorry you did not match to any position." I checked the phone to make sure it was mine. Then, I look around to see if there was someone else and I was merely snooping into their email. I checked the address line to make sure it was mine. The entire time my brain was asking incredulously, "who is this email for?" Certainly, not me! It had to be a mistake.

I waited for another email to come through saying otherwise. I waited and refreshed my browser. And waited…and refreshed… and waited… reality started to kick in. So, all my years of schooling were for naught? The crippling student loans awaiting payment a wasted investment? A lifelong dream just dead with one sentence? I have never hit rock bottom in my life. It takes a lot for me to cry, but I crawled into a ball and once that first tear broke free, the rest poured out in loud uncontrollable heart-wrenching sobs. In fact I didn't just sob, I wailed and the tears flowed in an unbroken stream enough to fill the Zambezi River. I saw my world come to a standstill. It felt like there was a storm and complete darkness. All I'd ever yearned for was to become a Medical Doctor. How could this be? I was faced with one of the most difficult conundrums in my life and I was helpless. Even worse, thinking of my parents' disappointment kept sending rivulet of tears streaming down my cheeks. I wept!

During the ensuing days, I spiraled into a deep depressive funk. I didn't want to eat. Who needed food when I had bouts of crying three times a day like 3 square meals? I didn't even want to talk to friends and family. Who needed to hear their corny albeit well-intentioned motivational speeches on handling disappointments? As for social media, it was a no-go zone. I refused to see the rest of my cohort in merriment while all around me my world was crashing. Within me, my heart was breaking with every stroke of the clock. I was broken.

Remember the clinical rotation I had committed to while awaiting Match Day? I had to carry on. While in medical school we had been taught about the nobility of the physician's call where the patient precedes self. Going in each day as if nothing had happened was torture. A plastic smile pressed on my lips; my voice, high-pitched with forced cheerfulness; my heart desperately yearning for something to ease the ache, yet I trudged through. After work, I'd head straight away to my local church. Some days I would pour my heart out to God in prayers and hymns. Yet other times, the pain would be so heavy that all I could do was sob and clean the pews with the flow of my tears.

In one of my days of self-pity, I was hit with the memory of my favorite wise saying by my grandmother *"little by little said the thoughtful boy, moment by moment I will try."* She always reiterated to me the importance of never giving up, of trying repeatedly until every feasible option was exhausted. With those words ringing in my head, I picked myself up and did something about my dilemma. I began contacting every medical connection I had or had encountered. Many proved to be dead ends but I didn't let that deter me. I kept at it.

      Meanwhile, my roommate from medical school, sweet Niti, reached out to me. She had matched into a program in New York but was concerned about my plight. Trying to proffer a solution, she immediately put me in contact with another friend of hers who had failed to match a few years back. He graciously shared with me his resume and advised that I format mine likewise and send to all programs I could in the US.

      I got to work! Even while acknowledging the likely futility of applying again after the initial rejection, I carried on. I would send out over 400 emails each week and would receive a slew of rejection letters from residency programs, but also about 25-50 failed email delivery. The cycle continued the following week, and the next, until Memorial Day rolled in May.

      Sometime that Monday, to take my mind off my predicament, I paid a visit to my friend Ebot in Maryland. Usually I will spend the night at her place, but for some reason I insisted on driving back home late to York, PA. The one-hour drive, in the still of the night, was soothing and helped to ease my broken heart albeit fleetingly. When I got home, I felt unusually energized and my spirits were uplifted. I can now attest it was all God's will for the spirit to lead me back home that night for in spite it being so late, I found myself sitting in front of my computer to send out emails to more residency programs. This time around, I did something different. I sifted through the failed delivery emails to further probe why they were undelivered. There were about 25-50 of them in number. I created a separate folder, and went through their respective hospital websites to update the failed delivery email addresses with the correct email addresses. With these new updated email addresses, I sent off another set of emails hoping that something will come of at least one and off to sleep I went.

Mind you, graduation day was coming up June 16 and I had no plan in sight. However, I was determined to stick it out to complete the journey. On Thursday May 31, I was at the hair salon. As I sat there idle while my tendrils enjoyed the greasy caress of my coiffeuse, I started fidgeting with my phone and scrolling through the emails on my blackberry. Suddenly, I saw this lone email highlighted HIGH PRIORITY. I started reading, "we would like to invite you…" I blinked, read again… The words began to record in my head from my eyes, accelerating the already rampant pounding of my heart against my ribs. Ah! This couldn't be real! Should I jump? Should I scream? Should I cry? Well, you better believe I did all three! I screamed so loud running out of the Salon to the road. Immediately I called my mum and we sure blew each other's ears with louder screams as I continued my happy dance on the street.

Visa complications had forced a foreign candidate in the McLaren internal medicine program in Flint, MI to drop out at the last minute. I was given three days to come in for the interview. Although this was a long way from home, it didn't matter for even wild horses couldn't keep me away. I showed up bright and early on that fateful day; one of six candidates all vying for the one lone spot. With the words of my uncle, Ngole, "never be afraid to fail" ringing in my head, I strutted in confidently knowing that this could be the only shot I got to secure placement. I hadn't quite driven off the parking lot when I got the call confirming my acceptance into the program.

For the last time I cried, but this time in relief, in happiness and in gratitude for unwavering faith during adversity. For family, friends and colleagues who did not allow me wallow in unproductive despair. For the end of an ordeal, the fulfillment of a dream, and the start of a new career with endless possibilities.

Seven years later and with many professional accomplishments as an internist, my days of humble beginnings still invoke bittersweet memories. Sometimes in the stillness of time, I ponder on the lingering question: "what if I had never made it into a residency program? What would my story be now?" While I am ever grateful that I would never have to answer this question, I am aware that there are many medical school graduates who live this reality every day.

My story of not matching may have ended positively, yet there is still a lesson or two for those who ultimately do not match. Foremost, do not dwell on your grief. Do not let it consume you and never give up. Then, be flexible and figure out which part of your future is negotiable and which isn't. If you don't have a mentor, find one as their support and guidance during this time is invaluable. Most importantly if you believe in any higher power, then pray fervently and believe in your God. Believe in Him and let nothing deter your faith.

Truth is, at some point during my unmatched ordeal I stopped crying and started thanking God. I thanked him especially for the little things. For the ability to think and know I am thinking. For the ability to eat, taste, swallow and feel satisfied. For the ability to stand tall, walk without pain or any deformity. For the ability to be alive and living. I knew this temporary delay was setting the stage for one of his many testimonies of faith and boy o boy, did my God deliver! This is one resounding testimony of the power of God and I can and will never take it for granted.

From the modest origins of a Caribbean Medical school, a reject on Match Day, and eventually an internal medicine resident, I have since landed my dream job and I can proudly say, I get treated with the same respect as any of my colleagues who matched on Match Day. When a patient lays on a sick bed battling sickness, the least they care about is whether that physician attending to them had matched on Match day. All they care about is the physician's healing touch.

Failing to match into residency is a tough experience. But if a career in medicine is truly something you are passionate about; it should not stop you from pressing onward to achieve your goal. I hope my story will serve as a beacon of hope for those who are going through the process of not matching or who may someday go through the process or any other process of rejection. Mind you, this story is not an ode to my greatness. I was not a genius who did not match on Match day. I was just a regular student as many of us are. The sun shines far away even on cloudy days and when you least expect it a glimmer of light might burst through and brighten your day, this is true even for those who do not match on Match day.

ACKNOWLEGDMENT

For my angels whom I love so much, Bella Francesca, Veronique and Paula you are capable of amazing things.

Maureen Muke, MD

Maureen Muke, MD is a Board Certified Internist and Department Chair of Medicine at Mercy One in North Iowa, Mason City. Born and raised in Cameroon, Dr. Muke earned her Bachelor of Science degree in Biology in 2007 from University of Massachusetts, Boston. She went on to earn her prestigious medical degree with Honors in 2012 from the American University of Antigua College of Medicine. She completed her Internal Medicine residency at McLaren Flint, Michigan. Dr. Muke has been in clinical practice since 2012.

In her spare time, Dr. Muke enjoys volunteering, cooking, basketball and soccer. Her passionate and holistic approach to patient care has led to her participation in many community outreach programs. Currently, she sits on the advisory board of The Iya Foundation, a non-profit organization that offers health education and medical assistance to thousands of renal patients in the USA, Nigeria, Ghana, Sierra Leone and her home country of Cameroon.
Dr. Muke and her husband, Paul, are proud parents of three lovely girls, Bella, Veronique and Paula.

Dr. Bi Akwen Tadzong-Fomundam

Board-Certified Preventive Medicine Physician

Against All Odds.

My name is Dr. Bi Akwen Tadzong-Fomundam, and I hail from Mankon-Bamenda, Cameroon. I am a Board-Certified Preventive Medicine Physician, with a pending certification in Lifestyle Medicine. I wear many hats and I am passionate about the things I do. I am a Christian, physician, wife, mother, daughter, sister, and friend. I have to walk and chew at the same time. Time neither waits for me nor negotiates with me. I also enjoy many things beyond practicing medicine; gardening, cooking, dancing, singing, watching movies, shopping, event and interior decorating, everything about aesthetics and colors, educating, empowering, advocating for others, engaging in mind changing discussions, and studying human behavior. I always fancy myself as a private investigator.

When I was a child, I never missed an opportunity to help someone in need. If anyone sustained an injury while working in the house or the yard, I tried to intervene in my own little way. It was clear to me and others that I wanted to take care of people. I was a kind, just, but very spirited child. I guess you could also call it a strong-willed child. I cannot imagine what it takes to raise one of my kind.

During my Anglo-Saxon themed education in Cameroon, I spent some years in boarding school. This was a badge of honor for most children growing up in my hometown. During these formative years, I experienced some intense verbal, emotional, psychological abuse. The onslaught of the bullying stemmed from an unfortunate incident with the young lady assigned to care for me as an older sister in school. We called them "bigs." This recurrent bullying and abuse over 4 years came also from fellow students who loved and admired my big. They felt the need to right the perceived wrongs I had committed against my big. These events informed and shaped my life. I must point out I was just an immature ten-year-old child when these things started happening. Most of my errors and perceived failures stemmed from childish instincts and misrepresentation of facts by my peers. They did not warrant the aggressive response I got from so many fellow students and even some teachers. I learned to survive amidst heavy criticism and pain. I learned to not depend on others for support, and I developed a warrior spirit. Over the years, I realized that I had low tolerance for abusive people.

Looking back now, I hold no hard feelings, because I can see that my big and the people that were defending her were teenagers themselves and we all lacked the skills to handle certain challenges. We were just children trying to manage each other. I made it through these years, though not unscathed. Healing has been occurring in stages as new areas of emotional and psychological scarring become evident. Forgiveness has been a central theme in the healing process. This is in line with practicing lifestyle medicine.

I was enrolled to start school at the University of Yaounde (one of the few universities in Cameroon) in the fall of 1994 but those plans fell through due to an ongoing strike with no clear end in sight. My parents explored other options for my undergraduate education. A relative was visiting from the U.S.A. and offered to file a Form I-20 at one of the community colleges for me. It was a successful process, and I was now eligible to apply for a student visa. I remember praying and fasting before going to the United States Embassy in Yaounde to request a student visa. Everything went smoothly, and I was told to come back later in the day to pick up the visa. This was in January of 1995.

After obtaining my visa, my parents hurried to send me off. The Douala airport is about five to six hours away from my hometown, Bamenda. Most people travel the day before their flight to avoid traffic in the city, and to ensure a timely check-in at the airport. I was no different. Family, friends and well-wishers, came to bid me farewell at a send-off party my parents had organized. It was an emotional experience, but the future seemed exciting. We travelled to Douala and spent the night at a hotel.

On the morning of my departure, my parents sat next to each other, laid this semi-adult child across both pairs of laps and prayed for me. They spoke blessings into my life. At the end, they gave me their short but legendary lecture; "Your education is your father, your mother, your brother, your sister, your spouse and your friend. Even when all these people leave you, you will still have your education. If you get a good education, it will sustain you across nations, continents, and cultures. It will open doors for you wherever you find yourself. We are throwing you into the ocean of life, and you can either swim or drown, but the choice is yours."

In retrospect, I will say my parents were very brave; while they were both well-travelled, they had never been to the U.S.A. However, they had the faith, audacity, courage, hope and love to send their young daughter off to this strange land of promise to forge a future for herself. They felt confident that they had equipped me to face the world, and while I was young, I was up to the task. They had done the same for my elder brother a year earlier, and he seemed to be holding up pretty well.

My first flight ever was uneventful until we got to the Charles de Gaulle Airport in Paris. We had terrible turbulence because of severe weather conditions (heavy rains, high winds and lots of snow). As we later found out, most other flights had been re-routed to other adjacent airports, but our pilot exercised his skill set. When we touched down, I was emotionally wasted, but we gave the pilot and crew a standing ovation. At that moment, I wondered what I had gotten myself into, if this was how my life would end, and if I was better off going back home and ending all the distress. Thankfully, I had two uncles who were on the flight, and they both helped me through the turbulence and with getting on my connecting flight to Los Angeles. I remain forever thankful for all these little but tremendous blessings.

When I landed in Los Angeles, I was taken aback by the level of aggression that the customs agents displayed. They tore through all my property, bombarded me with questions, and took a lot of stuff with no explanation or intention to return them. I felt sad and lost. Coming from a culture where we did not ask a lot of questions, I kept my misgivings to myself, and desperately wished I had stayed back in my native land. I felt unwelcomed, and it added to all the other challenges I was about to face – separation from family, friends, support systems and all things familiar. I was about to be hit by a wave of culture shock, loneliness, and low-grade depression. Too many things were changing at the same time.

My cousin picked me up from the airport, and gave me my first home in this nation. Her husband set about getting me acclimated with the U.S.A., and making sure that I was enrolled in school. They gave me my first taste of fast food and American candy (I fell in love with Snickers). They had to teach me everything, including how to use the bus to get around and how to conduct myself. I got to taste pizza for the first time too, courtesy of my uncle and his fiancée – I thought it was disgusting the first time I ate it, but I refused to give up trying until I started enjoying it. I slowly settled in to my new abode and got about building my future. The beauty of youth is one's ability to adjust to or cope with changes in life. I made many new friends, enjoy Los Angeles, and start feeling whole again. I was surrounded by lots of family and friends who made me feel welcome and loved.

At the end of my first year here, I moved to the East Coast to join my elder brother. I was just getting comfortable in my new home when the move happened. It was disruptive, but became a blessing in disguise. It was a blessing because I needed to be close to my brother when things went wrong. Two months after my move, our family was hit with tragedy – my junior brother got killed in a car accident in Cameroon. This was the beginning of a painful and dysfunctional period in my life. The grief was sometimes unbearable, and I lost a grip on myself. For some time after this, I became undisciplined. I could not seem to pull myself together, and I came up with the most ridiculous coping mechanisms including overindulgence in food, retail therapy, and frequent crying spells. I engaged in a few pitiful dates too, thinking it would help with the healing process. I learned that it is a bad idea to date people at your most vulnerable moments. Thankfully, I never fell into more destructive coping habits that could have derailed my life.

For years after his death, there seemed to be a dark cloud over my entire family. This feeling of doom was exacerbated by the loss of other close family members including my uncle and grandparents. For my elder brother and myself, the pain was especially intense because we were unable to travel home to pay our last respects. We could not travel for financial reasons and for fear of losing our student status. I would say that being unable to lay close family to rest and pay last respects is the most difficult part of emigrating. You never quite have closure, and your imagination always runs wild. Sometimes, life absolutely feels like a mirage. You feel the absence of those you love, but you wonder if it is really true that they died, or if they just went on a long journey and lost contact with the family. I completed my undergraduate studies and was still as determined as ever to be a physician. I had faced and continued to face many obstacles due to my student status. International students tend to have fewer options on financing their education, especially when things go wrong with their original funding.

Registering for classes involved endless negotiations stemming from financial challenges; and there was constant pressure as one struggled to maintain a school-life-work balance. We came to the conclusion that we would not take no for an answer. In fact, it we considered it a travesty to take "no" as an answer from someone who did not have the authority to consider saying "yes." That meant we always negotiated our way up the authority chain until we could get a better answer from someone at the top.

Persistence never hurt either. We understood that in order to receive one must ask, in order to find one must seek, and in order to have a door opened, one must knock. These are some Biblical principles for life and they work. How long can anyone keep saying no to a person who needs a resource or an opportunity if they never stop asking? We tried as best as we could to be superhuman, but we were benefiting from the resilience of youth. Prayer, the word of God, and my faith have always been the most important things that helped me cope with all of life's curveballs while remaining confident that things will get better. Many times, I felt like giving up because I presumed the odds were hopelessly stacked against me, but my friends, and my biologic and church families would not let me throw in the towel. I had an army of people praying for, encouraging, supporting and sowing into my life. I considered myself blessed to have had a pastor and his wife who were very supportive, and who introduced us to a number of powerful men and women of God. The spiritual seeds sown into my life were life-altering. Even in life's most challenging circumstances, there is nothing that supersedes being around the right people at the right time and in the right places. After all, God uses human beings to accomplish His goals on earth. I am immensely grateful to all these people for not letting me give up on myself.

Getting into medical school posed another challenge because the process was not only expensive, but most schools would not even consider an international student. My first attempt at the Medical College Admission Test (MCAT) and medical school admission were unsuccessful. It was a very discouraging experience and season. As the weeks went by, I did not see any point in trying again because I could not see any light at the end of the tunnel. I had slowly allowed negativity to claw at my hopes and dreams. Viewing a setback (temporary condition) as a failure (chronic condition) can destroy one's vision and mindset. It is easy to start feeling like a victim of circumstance.

One day, I had a meltdown, but this was really my rock bottom in that season. I cried so hard and wondered why my life was so difficult. I did not understand why I could not seem to catch a much-needed break or breath of fresh air in my life. The truth about life is that when you hit rock bottom in any situation, the only other direction you can go (if you keep trying) is upwards. My brother had a conversation with me, and we called my pastor's wife. She prayed for me, spoke words of encouragement, and asked me to do my part. She was confident that God had not forgotten about me. If I did not do the things I was responsible for doing, then I was inadvertently disqualifying myself for a blessing. One always has to be willing to take that step of faith, even when all hope seems lost.

This is the key to moving beyond life's challenges. Setbacks are normal and important milestones, but those who accomplish their goals are simply those who refuse to give up or take no for an answer. They learn important lessons during their setbacks, and use them to spring forward. I got back to studying and re-applying to various medical schools. I saw a school counselor, asked many questions, and sought the advice of friends on which schools would most likely accept a foreign student. I ended up with a few interviews, and I got accepted into the first school that interviewed me. What a relief! I did not need to spend more money that I did not have. It had taken all the resources my brother's family and myself could muster to get me to my interview. I cancelled all my subsequent interviews. The next challenge was how to get a student loan as a foreign student. Thankfully, a kind and generous friend of my parents (who was also a physician) co-signed a loan for me. After my first semester in medical school, my change of status application was granted, so I could get the international student admissions office off my back and regularize my student loans. I worked in the sleep lab at my medical school to supplement my finances.

I had developed a new problem, and little did I realize what a nemesis it will become. I did well in undergraduate because of the testing format. Once I started taking multiple choice type tests, I could not perform at my best. The first time I noticed this problem was when I took the MCAT, but things gradually worsened after I got into medical school. This slowly but surely eroded my confidence and caused me to develop exam anxiety. This meant that I literally had little to no sleep on the night before any exam. It became a domino effect; pre-exam anxiety, poor rest, exam-day fatigue, suboptimal performance, repeat the cycle. I could not figure out how to break this vicious cycle. There was a significant difference between my knowledge base and my performance. I sought help from my professors and the school, but I kept getting redirected to the next person. I found myself on a wild goose chase so I let go. I had to overcome this nightmare on my own. It took a long time, and I paid a hefty price tag, but I learned a lot about vicious cycles and how to help others deal with them. It was a lesson in brokenness, humility, compassion and healing.

In retrospect, I always find it amusing that because I had always been considered brilliant, no one could imagine the agony I was going through as my test-taking challenges mounted. I could not convince most people who watched me grow up that I was facing academic challenges due to testing problems. It is very difficult to be compassionate or empathetic if one has not been humbled by life's challenges.

In January 2003, another tragedy struck during my second year of medical school. My best friend, who was pregnant at the time, died of extensive second and third degree burns after a domestic dispute incident. This was a culmination of months of verbal, emotional and psychological abuse at the hands of her husband. She had just moved out of their home, and returned to check on her daughter the day she was burnt to death. She was barely in her mid-twenties and left a three-year-old daughter behind. I had visited her a few months earlier in England, and came away with the opinion that she and her husband were in a very dysfunctional relationship that needed to go through a major crisis in order for things to change for the better. Never in my wildest dreams did I think she would not make it out alive. Her death remains a sore point for me. For all of us who knew and loved her, it was a powerful reminder that getting married to the wrong person could cost you your life.

It will be unfortunate to exclude racism from my experience in medicine. It is a sad reality. It is also very difficult to talk about racism because people have found ways of being racist without making it so obvious. Healing will only come when we become honest about what is going on and how we can right the wrongs or injustices that are being directed at subsets of our population. The truth will set us free when we decide to seek it and embrace it. There were many incidents during medical school, residency, and even practice that struck me as racist, but they were subtle. I will talk about the more obvious situations.

We had evidence-based learning sessions in the second year of medical school, during which patient cases were presented and we had to work our way through them in small groups. It became a pattern that black women were always presented as ignorant, uneducated, uncultured and poor single parents, while other races had more responsible portfolios. This had been happening for years, and it subtly fit the misconception that black people are inferior and chronic underperformers. We had to bring this to the attention of the school administration. They held meetings with most of the black students to discuss this racial misrepresentation in patient cases. The school finally agreed to re-write their patient cases so that all races will be equally represented in all socio-economic classes.

During one of my medical school rotations at a Family Practice clinic in Elizabethtown, Pennsylvania, I had a clear brush with racism. One of my patients, a five-year-old white male, refused to let me examine him. He stated that he did not want a black person to touch him. I informed my preceptor and she was embarrassed. It was clear by the blush on her neck and face. I was not offended, but I felt sorry for the child. A child that age is too young to be racist, unless they have been taught by their parents. The sense of sorrow I felt was because I realized this child's mind and experiences were being ruined before he had real exposure to life. He will grow up deprived of the joys and blessings of meeting and knowing good people of all races and creeds. The parents were apologetic, but I did not pay them much attention. I have come to the conclusion that devaluing a subset of human beings, not only exposes the insecurities of the perpetrator(s), but it results in the devaluation of all human beings. Nobody is ever safe in the hands of a hateful person. The good news is, love always overpowers hate.

I attempted dating an old friend during medical school, but things never worked out. The conflicts always stemmed from my Christian beliefs. I finally decided that I had to wait on God to bless me with a worthy husband. I had zero interest in dating and in the associated drama. I needed a husband, not a boyfriend or date. I needed a mature man, not a boy. I got out of any dating and remained single. Some friends made fun of me when I told them I was waiting on a blessing from God, but bless me He did. It did not happen immediately though. I got a gentle reassurance during one of my quiet prayer sessions with my heavenly Father. This has always been the key for me. Every time I get this gentle personal reassurance from God that my particular prayer point has been addressed, I stop worrying or wondering. God has always come through for me.

Meeting my husband was a reunion of sorts. We attended boarding school together as teenagers, and had always been cordial towards each other. However, neither one of us were thinking about dating. I was a tomboy who grew up only with brothers, and he was the class "Einstein" who seemed oblivious to the happenings around him. We met ten years later through his mother, and quickly connected on various levels. He was the answer to my prayers, and he proposed a few weeks after we started talking. This was what I had prayed for. I was interested in courtship, not dating. The complicating factor was distance. He was an elite U.S.- trained soldier who was toiling about three thousand miles away in the remote parts of Cameroon, and I was completing my last year of medical school. Communications were sporadic depending on his access to network while in the bushes. But he was a committed Christian just like myself, and we were walking a similar path in life.

We got married a year after I graduated from medical school with pomp and circumstance. The first few months of our marriage were heart-wrenching because my husband had to go back to service, and I was a newlywed "single" if that makes any sense. He had been planning to leave service once his contract was up, and getting married made him even more determined to do so. My husband did not renew it, but quietly left Cameroon before anybody could question his actions.

Getting married came with its own set of complications, specifically dealing with challenging in-law situations. I will say that life is full of curveballs, and one ought to keep praying for wisdom, endurance, grace, and sound judgment. Marriage and childbearing during residency are feats that will wear even the toughest person down. I realized that there would never be a good time as a female physician to get in the family way, so we expanded our family. Our first child was born a little over a year after our wedding.

Thankfully, while I was trying to figure out which career path to pursue after giving up my first love (surgery), I did clinical research for 3 years. This gave me some quality time with the family. My husband was completing his graduate studies, and committed to being a hands-on father to our young daughter. My second pregnancy became a life-threatening ruptured ectopic. The cause was unclear because I had no known risk factors. I had to undergo an emergency salpingectomy. Technically, my fertility was now cut in half besides the fact that I was racing against the proverbial clock. I loved children and wanted to have a few more. Nothing happened until the most inopportune moment of course.

Our family continued living in Maryland when I went to complete a residency in Internal Medicine in New York city. When I was not working or had a "golden weekend," I hopped on one of the myriads buses in Manhattan and headed to Maryland to spend time with my family. This was the most sensible option, because I did not care to own or drive a car in New York city, and I was unwilling to drive while exhausted. A weekend was called golden if you got Saturday and Sunday off. This was a special event in the life of a resident, because the most this could happen was once a month. I spent all my time at home cooking and freezing food so my family will be taken care of until I could make it back home.

During my first few months of medical internship, I got pregnant with my second child. I guess I was multitasking again. I later developed gestational diabetes, which multiplied my level of stress. I did not get any modifications to my schedule, so by the sixth month, I was scheduled to do a month of night float. Sleepless nights and pregnancy do not go well together. Between keeping my Obstetric, Endocrinology, and bi-weekly ultrasounds appointments and whatever else was thrown my way, I was already stretched thin.

Most of my fellow residents made things even harder by their unkind words and actions. They always insinuated that I was at fault for getting pregnant during residency. Little did they know that I was running on a limited tank and that this was a blessing I could not jeopardize. They did not care how I fared, and they got angry if they had to cover for me because I refused to unnecessarily expose my baby to radiation in the imaging suites. The residents could not seem to make up their minds – they grumbled when I could not run fast enough to night codes, but they asked me not to bother when they saw my bulging abdomen. After going through these conflicts for a while, I decided to stay strong and engaged. I showed up for codes and did my share of chest compressions during cardiopulmonary resuscitations. When some senior residents complained, I asked them to back off. I was sick and tired of listening to them speaking from both sides of their mouths. If I became the next code, then they will have to answer for it.

When fellow residents get angry with you, they resort to bullying, character assassination and other nefarious behaviors. Unfortunately for them, I was familiar with these antiques and I was ready to push back. That notwithstanding, it is another stressor on anybody, but most especially a pregnant woman. For a bunch of people practicing medicine, their lack of empathy and compassion was glaring. What these adults forget to understand is that for any child to be born, some woman has to sacrifice and pay a price. Most pregnancies are not convenient. They are a part of life. Professional women should not be punished or mistreated because they want to be good wives and mothers. We are excellent at doing multiple things and doing them well. We bring special skills to the table too.

Because of all the pressures I experienced, I started having premature labor contractions towards my seventh month of pregnancy. They started when I took stairs, so I switched to using elevators. Then they started showing up when I was walking briskly, so I slowed down my walk. The contractions became more frequent, to the point where standing up was enough to induce them. My program director, who had been my sole and avid protector, asked me to consider taking time off until the baby came. I declined. That was on a Friday. By the next Monday, I was ready to take him up on his offer. My condition had significantly worsened, and during one of my night shifts, I had to call out and get admitted to the Labor and Delivery Unit for monitoring. I refused to further jeopardize my baby's wellbeing to satisfy my career pursuit.

Aside from being pregnant, medical training is a force to be reckoned with. It is grueling, unforgiving, unrelenting, and a lot of times, outright abusive. Everything is put on the chopping block, including personal wellbeing, rest, proper nutrition, close relationships, and one's human dignity. The hours of training are long and endless, and sometimes disorienting to a human being. It is therefore not surprising that most people going through medical training recurrently suffer from low grade depression, anxiety and sometimes self-hate. You love medicine, but hate what is takes to become a physician.

There are few resources to deal with these problems, because we are supposed to be strong and resilient. When such resources are available, we avoid them like the plague because of the potential for lifetime stigma and career stifling. We suffer in silence, and a lot of fellow physicians resort to crazy or covert stress management tools.

It is disheartening that the people that are being trained to care for others are deeply victimized by the system that trains them. No wonder young people who had lofty ideas of helping other human beings when they enrolled in medical school become some of the most jaded, withdrawn, inconsiderate and cynical professionals you meet. The health of physicians is just as important as the health of their patients. Broken doctors are not very helpful to their patients because you cannot give what you do not have. Current statistics indicate that we lose about 400 physicians to suicide annually. Physicians also have a significantly higher rate of suicide than the average population. Shamefully, there is no concerted effort to track or manage this problem, because it requires a broken healthcare training and delivery system to be drastically restructured.

After returning from a peaceful maternity leave, I found myself in the claws of two lazy and complaining residents. These were my colleagues in training, and they were 4 months ahead of me due to my recent maternity leave. I was abused and misused because I was neither an intern (a first-year resident) nor a full resident. I was given responsibilities without privileges. It was a traumatizing, yet important learning experience. At the end of the year, I had to admit that I was never cut out to be an Internist. I could not imagine myself doing this for the rest of my life. I wanted out, and my Program Director gave me a gracious exit and genuine support.

My year may have seemed wasted, but it paved the way for a new pursuit, Preventive Medicine. As the Bible states in Romans 8:28, all things always work together for good to those that love God and are called according to His purpose. I got into a program in Upstate New York, and this transformed my whole concept of medicine. The Preventive Medicine program involved not only doing rotations, but also completing a Masters in Public Health degree. It was a wide-ranging and enriching program.

Against all odds, I got pregnant with baby number three during this training. Another season with a new set of challenges. I was already managing two children, one of whom had speech delay and needed extensive early childhood intervention services. During the first trimester, I fell out of favor with a female professor because I kept falling asleep during her class. She wrote unkind reviews about me, but the saving grace was that I kept getting some of the best exam scores in her class. I apologized to her multiple times as I explained my predicament, and while she claimed to understand, her attitude was unrelenting. Eventually, we agreed that I will stand up and walk around in her class every time I felt sleepy. When the baby came along, another professor penalized me for turning in a paper one week late. My baby was born the weekend the paper was due. I got to work on it as soon as I left the hospital, but that was not enough. However, I look at these things as the price you pay for what you want. Things should be kept in perspective. I share these events, not to evoke a pity party, but to draw back the curtains on the challenges we have to face just like everyone else. We have to find good ways to cope and thrive, while always striving to put our best feet forward.

When anyone sets out to live a meaningful life, challenges are to be expected - adversity is an integral part of life although it can erode some of the buoyancy and optimism of youth. Amid adversity, I am choosing to take control of the situation, learn all that I can, and move forward better, stronger and wiser than I was. Most of life's outcomes do not depend on what went wrong, but on how you managed the challenges you faced. Good mentoring is critical during such seasons.

It took a very long time for me to fully realize and embrace my calling in Medicine. Everything came into focus in 2013 when I won the Gold Humanism Honor Award in Medicine. It was a pleasant surprise, but it brought to my attention what I have been doing well and how to polish up that talent. My goal is to break down the complexities of medicine for my patients, while constantly applying motivational interviewing techniques to move them from a place of complacence, to a place of action and full engagement. We have to change the way we communicate with our patients, so that our messages are not lost in translation.

Regarding personal and professional development, I think I have learned a lot of valuable lessons along my unconventional career and life path and I will share a few below. They also are the tools I use when managing my patients, because most human health challenges are associated with lifestyle and choices. My mantra is that lifestyle is the key to enhancing vitality and health through education, empowerment and advocacy. I have become extremely passionate about lifestyle management, because it is the only sustainable and safe way to promote health. It focuses on the whole human being, not just body parts or systems. I need to prime my patients to take charge of their lives and health, stop playing victim, and join me in the quest for better health for all. Health as eloquently defined by the World Health Organization, 'is a state of complete physical, mental and social well-being and not merely the absence of disease or infirmity.'

- Distill everybody to a human being. This simplifies and clarifies everything. When in doubt, do an honest assessment of what drives any human behavior.

- Maintaining success is more challenging than achieving it because your talent can always take you to a place where your character cannot sustain you. When you find yourself on an upward trajectory in life, work more diligently on fine-tuning your character. Bad character will sabotage or destroy every good thing you accomplish.

- Avoid familiarity with the people around you. Familiarity breeds contempt, guaranteeing that you will undermine the gifts, talents, and amazing attributes of those you have become too familiar with.

- Privileges and responsibilities always go together. Accepting one without the other will set you up for failure.

- Apart from a sound knowledge base, respect and compassion should be the hallmarks of a good physician. As the old saying goes, people do not care how much you know until they know how much you care.

- Never exempt yourself from human suffering. It is the lot of mankind. Eventually, you will draw from the lot. Continue to exercise compassion and empathy towards others. You will need them at some point in life.

- The real character of a person is defined not by what they do when they are being observed or when they meet their match in life; it is defined by what they do in their hidden moments, or when they feel a real or perceived sense of unaccountability, invincibility or

impunity. What curbs human behaviors and tendencies is the fear of consequences.
- Practice makes perfect. Be careful what habits you are practicing or building. They will become a perfect stronghold.

- Whatever you feed will grow, and whatever you starve or malnourish will die. This is true for habits, knowledge, skills, relationships and just about everything else in life.

- Know and be true to yourself. It helps you position the people you allow into your life and space, and is critical to maintaining your peace, joy and sanity.

- Authenticity is a requirement for relevance. When an entity loses its authenticity, it immediately becomes worthless.

- Learn to manage your expectations. Do not ask for or expect from people what they cannot give you. Do not demand things from people that exceed their scope, capacity or ability. You will end up angry, frustrated, exasperated and disappointed.

- There is a difference between being nice and being kind. Nice is a superficial charm that you can turn on and off as needed, usually for selfish reasons. Good con people are some of the nicest people you will ever meet. Their niceness keeps you questioning your judgment of who they really are. Kindness is a more authentic, consistent, deep-rooted and character-based attribute. Kindness does not have any potential malice or deceit attached to it, and does not seek to harm or hurt.

- People are only as faithful as their options. Give people better options and you will most likely have better choices and outcomes. Therefore, policies play a critical role in curbing or creating social injustices or inequities.

- Freedom is over-rated and choice is under-rated. Freedom is not the right to be reckless, outrageous or wayward. It is the right to be the best you can be, because the world is waiting for you to deliver your gift. Choice means exercising your ability to make a good decision, no matter how small. Making good choices today will unlock more options for you in the future. Conversely, making bad choices today will limit your future options.

- Gratitude is the antidote to misery and pride. It allows you to find reasons to remain thankful and optimistic. It also reminds you that but for the grace of God, you could have found yourself in any undesirable position in life. No wonder the grace of God is called amazing, because it saved a wretch like me. I am thankful that God loved me enough to give up His precious Son for me.

I am thankful for those who have blessed me in the pathway of life; they have lightened my burdens and have provided welcome moments of relief and refreshment along the journey of life. So many people have blessed me in so many ways along this interesting path. I would never have made it this far without the contribution (no matter how great or small) of many people in my life. They know themselves, and I want to express my profound gratitude again.

I am thankful for those who have abused, betrayed, bullied, dehumanized, exploited, frustrated, humiliated, or hurt me. While the pain you caused may have been excruciating and sometimes debilitating, you forced me to learn and grow. You forced me to search myself, learn more about myself, and come up with tools for survival and self-improvement. In fact, most of the lessons I have gleaned in life have been from places of adversity and pain.

I have become a sensitive yet strong woman. I am sensitive to the needs, hurts, fears, challenges, and vulnerabilities of others. But you can bet I have developed a rugged and weather-beaten personality. I have learned the need for boundaries; they protect and optimize functioning and are not meant to serve as walls of isolation.

- Do not take hostages. You have to give up your own freedom and expend a lot of energy to keep a hostage. It stifles your growth and progress. Therefore, we must forgive and release others.

- Avoid the need to control others. It is more important to work on controlling yourself. Every time you try to control others, you are engaging in an exercise in futility. It is exhausting, stressful, frustrating and outright unproductive. You cannot control any body's behavior except yours.

My goal is to be a physician who practices medicine with a blend of compassion, wisdom, and scholarship in order to optimally treat each patient. I never want to miss an opportunity to be a blessing.

Acknowledgment
To all the people that have loved and cared for me throughout my journey.

Dr. Bi Akwen Tadzong-Fomundam

Bi Akwen Tadzong-Fomundam MD, MPH, is a Board-Certified Preventive Medicine Physician currently practicing as a Locum Tenens in South Carolina. Born and raised in Cameroon, she migrated to the United States in 1995. She obtained her Bachelor of Science in Biochemistry from University of Maryland at College Park in 1999. She earned her Medical Degree from Pennsylvania State Milton S. Hershey College of Medicine in 2005.

She did clinical research at Washington Hospital Center before proceeding to complete an Intern Year at New York-Presbyterian Queens. She completed residency in General Preventive Medicine combined with a Masters in Public Health degree at State University of New York, Buffalo in 2013. She has practiced in South Carolina and Indiana, with experiences in HIV care, primary care, house calls, and urgent care.

She is passionate about Lifestyle Medicine and coaching. She is a Christian who firmly believes that life works best on God's principles. Most human problems stem from our unwillingness to cooperate with these principles, and a fundamental misunderstanding of the gifts of freedom and choice. Lifestyle Medicine provides a sustainable and optimal pathway to good health and vitality, using the basic principles of life.

She has multiple interests in life, and refuses to settle for anything but excellence. She embraces every opportunity to add value to the lives of others.

She is a co-author of *Beyond Challenges*, the riveting life stories of fifteen African Immigrant Physicians and recipient of a Gold Humanism Honor Award in Medicine.

She is married with three children.

Dr. Shirley Ayuk-Takem, D.O
Board Certified in Internal Medicine and Critical Care Medicine

Saving lives every day, yet I couldn't help my own.

Achakasara

In the Bayangi language, *Achakasara* is a weed that can grow anywhere whether planted or not. It even grows on rocks: a resilient and hard to destroy plant. My extended family fondly calls me *Achakasara*. To childhood friends, I am Ma'Yese based on my prowess in "dodging" (dodgeball) and "seezo" (jump rope) in those days. To my immediate family, I am "Cheri coco" and to the government I am Shirley Ayuk-Takem.

I am board certified in both Internal Medicine and Critical Care medicine with a passion for disease prevention. Ever heard of an ICU physician whose goal in life is to keep people out of the ICU? Ironical right? Yes, but that's me. To many, I'm just a physician but outside of the white coat and underneath this brown skin lies so much more - the avid world traveler, adventure seeker, blogger, aspiring author, mystery book reader, a thrifty baller, aspiring pilot and passionate philanthropist.

As an Osteopathic physician, my thirst for the healing of the mind, body and spirit is insatiable. I am currently exploring eastern medicine and healing techniques to add to my repertoire of skills. Like my mother before me, I believe wholeheartedly that the futures of families, countries and the world depend on the education of the female child. Indeed, like someone once said, "to educate a woman, is to educate a nation".

My path towards becoming a physician was a convoluted one, filled with trials, tribulations, sacrifice, rejections, loss and ultimately success. Along the way, I have been humbled and have learned valuable lessons, benefited from the benevolence of strangers and basked in the grace, mercy and forgiveness of God. Most days I feel fortunate and blessed to be where I am, but occasionally I wonder if the sacrifice of my personal life and the singular tunnel vision pursuit of a career was worth it. So how did this all begin? How did I come to wear this albatross around my neck?

Speak your destiny into existence

Growing up as the youngest of five in Cameroon, West Africa, my childhood was idyllic. My parents were both professionals with advanced degrees and in their circle of friends were several physicians who served as role models. My US educated dad was a lifetime member of National Geographic Magazine, so we received a monthly publication. It was from these that three-year old Shirley learned to read. I have vivid memories of reading a story about American aviator, Amelia Earhart, around age five. So fascinated was I by her story that I told my dad about my life career dilemma; I wasn't sure if I wanted to be a physician or a pilot. Pragmatist that he was, daddy quizzed me on why those two were viable career choices and I gave him my reasons as best as a five-year-old could. His advice was "why don't you become a physician who flies planes when they're off?". And with that sentence at five years old, my career path was set. From that point on I immersed myself in my studies with the singular goal of being a Physician and helping heal people when I grew up. It also helped that I was naturally inquisitive and driven to crack puzzles as my early forays into Agatha Christie and Nancy Drew mysteries proved.

Beware of dream killers

By age 14, I was done with secondary school and eager to move to the US to join my siblings and start college. But my mom wouldn't have it; she wanted me to gain a little more maturity. Or maybe like any mother, she just wasn't ready to see the last of her brood leave the nest. Well two years later, she didn't stop my move when I graduated High School. I traded life in capital city Yaoundé, Cameroon for dorm life in Birmingham, AL, USA. And what a change it was- staying on my own for the first time, navigating a new educational system and culture, trying to be understood with a foreign accent and sometimes trying to understand the unusual accent of my peers, making new friends, fitting in, managing a budget…it was all so overwhelming.

In all these, my desire to become a physician still burned strong, a dream I decided to share with one of my college advisors. She scoffed, and with an incredulous look on her face and a matter-of-fact voice advised me to aim for something more attainable or feasible for someone from Africa. She was only doing me a favor to avoid disappointment and almost certain failure; she stated. It didn't matter to her that I was an excellent student who even started college as a sophomore; medicine was not for people like me. As I walked out of her office that fine September 1997 day, all I could say was "wow"! So Africans weren't cut out to be physicians. Well, she did her part in advising and I did mine in listening; didn't mean I had to adhere to anything she said. And that is exactly what I did in the ensuing semesters: visit with her per university protocol, have her sign-off on my courses and went on my merry way. I hadn't come here to let some stranger, even if well-meaning, kill my dream. No ma'am.

Mind you, she wouldn't be the only one to try to sway me. Many people tried and failed miserably and they came in all kinds of disguises as friends, strangers, relatives you name it. They all tried to shove down unsolicited advice down my throat when they felt I should be doing something different. Why not nursing like everyone else? Why must it be medicine? All these people were trying to Pidgeon-hole me into what they thought I should be doing with my life. No one ever bothered to ask me about what I wanted to be. I refused to let her or anyone else for that matter dampen my spirit. Here I was, a round peg that was being forced to fit into a square hole by everyone.

A dream delayed is not a dream deferred

Back in those days, the internet wasn't as easily accessible as it is today. I had no access at home so, I spent most of my free time in the library browsing the internet, researching and educating myself on what the MCAT was and all the requirements of getting into medical school in the US. I took the pre-med prerequisites and decided to use them to earn a Bachelor's of Science Degree in Respiratory Therapy. I figured, it would be nice to be in a hospital around doctors and patients while gaining any kind of medical experience and exposure and inching my way towards medical school.

But until then, there were bills to be paid and I had to work. First it was at a fast food restaurant and then an upgrade to the zoo. However, working and going to school during the day was taking a toll on me so; I took a 3-week Certified Nurse's Assistant (CNA) course and started working as a CNA at night while going to school during the day. It meant big bucks too for a college student like me - a whopping $7.10 per hour. Look at me! On my weekends off, I worked as a home health aide with the elderly and infirmed doing all the mundane tasks that no one wanted to take on. From scrubbing the toilet seat with a toothbrush, to cleaning the bottom of the pool even when I didn't know the first thing about swimming. Sometimes too, I served as chauffeur when I took my elderly patients grocery shopping. However, I was supposed to make sure that I parked far away and stayed out of sight. This was Alabama after all. To another, it might have been disconcerting, but to me it didn't matter, I was in survival mode. I had come to America for a greater conquest and even if it didn't come easy, I was going to conquer one way or another.

During my junior year, I was accepted to Medical school. I was ecstatic! But my joy was short lived. Without qualifying for financial aid, how was I going to pay my way through this expensive tryst? However, never one to easily give up, I pulled on my best Walmart chic suit and fancy Payless shoes to walk into every bank in Birmingham, AL in search of a student loan. It was a futile effort. Many days later, I grudgingly accepted defeat; medical school was going to have to wait- at least for now. With a heart heavy with pain, I let that admission go.

Hustle and flow

June 30, 2003, Jersey shore, NJ in all its familiar glory- happy families out picnicking, carefree children building sand castles, young coeds showing off well-earned summer bodies, orangey from a little too much tanning oil, sea gulls crying, eager waves cascading; an altogether tranquil time in a state not usually accustomed to tranquility. I was part of that carefree crowd celebrating my birthday and basking in my accomplishments. BS in Respiratory Therapy earned, and now a Registered Respiratory Therapist in Philadelphia, PA. I tell you; this wine cooler was very well deserved.

As I slipped away, I heard the distant ringing of my phone and it was my mother, unusually playful and light-spirited. She wished me a happy birthday, chatted with me, didn't for once tease me about getting married soon AND she told me how much she loved me. Hold on. Who is this woman and what have you done to my mother? But I had heard right; my mother said she loved me. Very much. Not that I ever doubted she did, but those words are ones that are rarely heard from the lips of an African parent. They'd gladly take a hit for you, sacrifice all they had just to make sure you lacked nothing, sleep hungry so you didn't have to, work in the heat and climb Kilimanjaro barefoot to give you the kind of life they only ever dreamed of. But to say that I love you? Never!

Especially not if that parent were my mother: long standing educator and known strict disciplinarian. The no-nonsense woman with a backbone of steel who in the throes of labor pain just before my birth, navigated a manual transmission Renault 18 through rocky unpaved roads decorated with grate sized potholes because her husband was away from home on assignment and unable to transport her to the nearest hospital to deliver. Dramatic? Find you an African mother or friend and you will find this very normal. And no, truly there were no functional ambulance services then; perhaps not even now. And it was this same woman who was now telling me how much she loved me. Yes, she was alright, no she didn't have a fever; she had never been better, she quipped when I jokingly asked her if she was alright. Did mummy really just say 'I love you"? Hmmm, okay… Stunned and still reeling from her unusual declaration of love, I promised to call her back when I returned to Philadelphia that evening.

Tragedy strikes

Back in Philadelphia, I tried for a few hours to reach her to no avail. I chalked it up to the usual network problems in Cameroon and went to sleep. Early the next day, I woke up with a phone call from my older sibling. Mom was dead. Killed by a drunk driver while running errands shortly after talking to me. Speechless and numb were the only emotions I remembered feeling and crying was the only activity I remember partaking in. Maybe I ate, maybe I slept, maybe I spoke to concerned sympathizers - I do not know. From sunrise to sunset I cried for a voice of reason, my tough disciplinarian, tough to please yet much too loving mother was gone too soon.

I managed to get myself together to fly out to Florida to spend time in mourning with my siblings. As the numbness ebbed, the anger set in. The woman who never consumed alcohol in excess carelessly killed by a drunk driver. You see she unfortunately wasn't wearing a seat belt; a common driving practice in that part of the world. So when she was T boned by the other driver, she was expelled through the windshield of her car, gashing her head on the tarred road surface. Still conscious though, she was at the time more worried about her chauffeur who was unconscious. But that was my mother for you; always more concerned by another's pain than hers.

Several onlookers gathered although in all honesty, it would have been better if they hadn't. Instead of helping, her purse was stolen. She was able to hail a cab to transport her driver and her to the nearest hospital. Again, no ambulances available. I guess even after three decades; some things just never change. At the first hospital, the CT scan was out of service. Typical. Another cab, another hospital. But here, she was refused service because she had no money; thanks to the "concerned" onlookers who had so conveniently helped themselves to her purse. Who steals from an injured accident victim? Beats me! She borrowed a phone and placed a call to my dad who immediately set out on his way. It would take him less than an hour to get there but before anything could be done for her, she died from her injuries. Just like that-a senseless death which could have been prevented in saner climes.

She was buried not long after, but I couldn't bring myself to attend her funeral. 16 years later, I am yet to look at the photos of my mother laying in a casket. My memories of my mother are of her walking and talking and I refuse to taint them with ones of her laying in a casket.

Making a dollar out of fifty cents

Following the death of my mother I pursued my physician quest with possessed zeal. No longer was it a leisurely stroll but a mad sprint towards the finish line. I shut down and shut myself in. Some of my pre-requisites were expiring, so I retook them. My MCAT had expired so I retook it. I was working two jobs, maintaining a fulltime academic load with classes spread across 3 campuses one of which was 100 miles away from home. Even sleeping became a luxury, but that was ok; there would be lots of time to catch up on sleep in the grave.

I finished retaking the pre-requisites and the MCAT and applied to several medical schools but only made it as far as the waitlist at some schools. Notwithstanding my high GPA, I had been out of school too long (5 years); and it was hard to convince the admissions' officers to overlook this academic gap. I was advised to go and apply to graduate school and reapply in 1-2 years. Also, they wanted traditional Biology/Chemistry pre-med students which I made the conscious choice not to be. I tried to explain to those people that it's not like I had spent the time off from school frying puff puff on the side of the street. During those 5 years, I had worked in several hospitals and gained valuable experience which could never be gained via formal education. You would think that should count for something. But no! Getting admissions officers to understand that was harder than growing waterleaf in the Sahara Desert.

During the interviews I managed to nab, I was advised to consider other viable options. Why not Nursing? There was a shortage of nurses, I was informed. What about becoming a Physician assistant? That was an up and coming field, I was advised. Those were both noble professions but, no thanks. They would have been better off saving their breath and the unsolicited advice. I didn't need it, and my resolve was not to be broken. By this time, I was accustomed to being told here in America that I wasn't good enough and certain dreams and career aspirations were not for people like me. That I needed to be more realistic. Instead of deterring me, this instead served to give me the extra motivation that I needed to prove them wrong! I learned that it didn't matter what people thought about you or believed about you as long as you believed in yourself. Till date, I am saddened by how these people charged with the duty of shaping young minds so easily misuse that office to kill, instead of nurture the dreams of young hopefuls from underrepresented groups. Who knows how many dreams like mine have been killed by such negativity of pseudo wisdom?

Scared to gamble by waiting to see if I would be taken off any of the waiting lists in time for a Fall start, I kept looking. In late January and down to my last $300, I saw an ad for a Doctor of Osteopathic Medicine school in Arizona. It was already close to the deadline but on a whim, I rushed to apply. A few weeks later, I was invited for an interview at the least opportune time. I was regularly working 2 to 3 jobs but everything I made had gone out to endless application fees and interview costs. I was flat out broke; no money even to pay the looming February bills. So now, would I be getting a plane ticket or paying some of the said bills to keep late charges and creditors at bay? The plane ticket won.

Speak your dreams into existence:

With barely enough money in my pocket to splurge on a hot sandwich, I landed in Phoenix, AZ. I had just enough money for either a hotel room or a rental car, but not both. So, I chose to shuteye on the hard airport benches and quickly freshened in the public bathroom before stepping out for my first real view of Phoenix.

From the moment I drove out of the airport, a sense of calm came over me. I immediately knew that I belonged there! Something just felt right about everything. When I pulled into the campus, those feelings were re-affirmed. The people were friendly, warm and welcoming. The atmosphere was comforting; nothing like the icy coldness of some of the other medical schools I had visited. This was the place for me.

It was supposed to be an all-day affair, after which your application went to a committee which was meeting a few weeks later. We were told that we would be notified of their decisions 3-4 weeks after the interview. But one hour after my recorded interview began, there was a knock on the door. My interviewer left the room and went outside for a few minutes. He returned shortly to inform me that my interview was over. My heart sunk. Not again please, not again!

What did I do wrong? Maybe I had been too relaxed and casual; a little forward in letting my spunky personality show perhaps? But that was only because I immediately felt comfortable. Yes, I hadn't answered the questions with the typical pre-scripted answers and had instead drawn from my experiences in life and healthcare to give truthful answers. That wasn't so bad, right? Over the loud thud of my heartbeats, I barely heard the door reopen to the Medical school dean. My first thought was to apologize and ask if I had done anything wrong, but all I got was a smile. Everything was right, too right actually. I had been accepted on the spot! Check me out squealing in excitement. Finally!

For the rest of the day I was caught between joy and sadness. Joy for obvious reasons, but sad because my mother would never celebrate this day with me. She had been one of my biggest cheerleaders fueling my drive perhaps because like me; she had once nursed the dream of becoming a physician. But she was born in different times- the 50s, when the African society didn't place much stock on the education of the girl child. Her father would concentrate on the education of his sons; some of whom went on to obtain PhDs. But as the girl, my mother only had two career options: teaching or nursing and she chose the former.

My relentless drive towards a career in medicine had been for me as much as it had been for her. Later that evening I was back on a flight to Philadelphia to work my 11pm-7am shift. Those bills still had to be paid. While in Philadelphia, I received the official call from the admissions office notifying me that I had been accepted and that I would receive a scholarship. Finally, after being told no and maybe so many times I was finally getting an absolute YES with a scholarship to top it all off. Surreal!

The struggle is real

If I thought my troubles were miraculously over with admission, I was in for a rude awakening. There were expensive books to be bought, $2500 to be shelled out for the mandatory computer, a deposit to be made to hold my seat in the class and lots of other incidental expenses I hadn't anticipated when I painstakingly drafted my tight moving budget.

For example, who knew my car could guzzle up so much gas between Philadelphia to Phoenix? Right outside of St Louis, Missouri I was already short of gas money and had to call on family who rallied and bailed me out. Ever the penny pincher, I gave up motels for fitful naps at rest stops along the way.

Upon arrival in Phoenix, I couldn't afford to pay my deposit for an apartment and my last paycheck from Philadelphia was a week away. At least I had my car; and it became my own mobile home. After gaining the trust of the campus security guard, I slept in my car in 115-degree weather on campus for almost a week until my paycheck came through from Philadelphia. At night I was sweating like a pig in my cramped car as thoughts of impending rapists and serial killers clouded my mind. But come morning; I was in the public restroom refreshed and went on my day, chirpy as any other dreamy new student.

Accommodation finally sorted and then came the financial aid hassle. Apparently, I had made "too much money" the prior year to qualify for financial aid. Who knew? I remember being poorer than a rural church rat yet uncle Sam classified me as rich? Well, that was then, this is now; I no longer made that kind of money and I needed financial aid desperately. But bureaucrats are slower than snails, I tell you. It took 6 good months to finally get the powers-that-be convinced that I was no longer working at that job and was now a full-time medical student.

In the meantime, the school gave me small loans to sustain myself while the appeals process went through and I was able to pay my rent. I lived boarding school style with just running water. No electricity, no furniture, bare pantry. Nothing fancy; Just a roof over my head until my financial aid came through in December. But it was a huge upgrade from my mobile home/car of that first week, I must admit.
I would walk to school at 6 am to save on gas and avoid the heat and left campus at 11 pm when the library closed. It was cooler then (80 degrees). Being away from home all day too meant I wouldn't have to contemplate my lack of electricity too much. I ate all my meals on campus as we were constantly being fed by various entities that solicited our services upon graduation. By the time my financial aid finally came through in December, I had grown so accustomed to being penniless that I didn't even see any real need for change. My only splurge was to get electricity in my apartment. Other than that, nothing else really changed.

A series of unfortunate events

Before I knew it, clinical rotations in Alabama and medical school were over, and I found myself in Detroit; accepted to one of the top 5 DO IM programs in the country. I was interning at a busy suburban hospital where 20 admissions a night split between two interns meant a very slow evening. Some of the seniors had a saying, call if you need anything, but calling is a sign of weakness.

It was a January night as cold as any, but busier than most even for my high traffic hospital. It was a night of nonstop admissions, running rapid responses and code blues for us interns with supervision from the seniors. Apparently, we were being taught to learn to swim with the Piranhas. Sharks were docile in comparison. My cellphone had been going off nonstop too and messages were coming in back to back. I never even had time to look at the phone all through the night.

6 am found me in a patient's room running a code blue with backup from my senior and just when I was about to pronounce the patient dead and stop all resuscitative efforts, I pulled my cellphone out to see how long we had been coding the patient for. It was then that I saw all the messages that had come through. The top one said "call home, dad has had a stroke"! Immediately, I froze and lost all ability to think. I asked my senior to take over and ran out of the room. Frantically, I called my siblings to see what was going on and then called Cameroon. It was then that I found out that my dad had fallen on his way to the bedroom the night before, so relatives helped him to his bed. It was only when he awoke the next morning, unable to speak and move one side of his body that they realized that he had suffered a stroke and that was probably what led to the fall. He was taken to his Cardiologist in Yaoundé' who correctly diagnosed the stroke, ordered a CT scan of the head and told him to follow up with a neurologist the following week. I was infuriated! You don't have a stroke and be told to go home and follow up in a week. He needed to be in a hospital. What were they thinking? In retrospect though, perhaps he was better off at home.

What ensued was a series of unfortunate events. He was taken to the hospital where his BP meds were resumed. Consequently, his BP dropped, and the stroke effects worsened. In quick response, my siblings flew home to help him stabilize in the hope of bringing him back to the US for more advanced treatment. There were no physical or occupational therapists readily available so my sister tried to do range of motion exercises on him much to the chagrin of the pompous nurses who scolded her for exercising him. She relented and his rigidity and contractures worsened.

A host of doctors saw him; each one leaving with a new prescription for him to take. Quite interesting is the fact that some of these prescriptions are written for medications that could only be filled at a particular pharmacy either owned by the physician or with which they had affiliations. Many tests were written, most of them duplicates and only meant to be done in clinics affiliated by the authorizing physicians. Nurses had the opportunity to have their cut too. The prescriptions could very well be filled but never seen by the patient. The savvy nurses simply diverted it for private sale to earn a decent profit. Welcome to the business of healthcare in Cameroon.

In a 4-day period, my daddy was ordered 3 echocardiograms. I spoke to my sister daily and got updates and wrote progress notes daily like he was a patient of mine. I'd then go over my notes with my residency program director who was an angel and a godsend. Not once did she complain about my obsessive questioning.

I was obsessed with writing these notes and trying to help manage and guide my father's care but there was no reasoning with some of the doctors managing his care. It was then that I started to realize that we would have been better off keeping my dad at home and hiring a live-in nurse for him, my program director and I could have very well managed his care from the US.

Not only was I a daughter but now a tele-doctor to my father. His condition worsened; he became septic and was transferred to the ICU where he went into cardiac arrest. No amount of coding could resuscitate him and on Monday January 21st, 2013, daddy went to meet his ancestors. And just like that my siblings and I became orphans.

A few years later, I completed my Internal medicine residency and did a Critical care medicine fellowship. Sadly, both of my parents, who had been my loudest supporters all through my long rocky journey were absent in all my celebratory photos. As a physician, I have taken care of more accident and stroke patients than I can count. Heck, on the day that my father died I admitted 2 stroke patients and they all walked out of the hospital with minimal disabilities. Yet, both of my parents walked into hospitals on both legs and left lifeless on a gurney. Life sucks!

For many years I was bitter about the senseless death of both of my parents - the unfortunate victims of a broken healthcare system. But one day I woke up and realized I was tired of being angry and bitter, especially when those negative emotions eating at me could never bring them back. Besides, what would these two selfless people have wanted? For me to funnel that pain into power. And that is exactly what I did.

These days, I strive to change the negative impact of being in the ICU into a positive one for my patients and their families. Emotionally, it is rewarding to see hope overshadow the fearful stare, a smile break behind the tears and calm replace the frantic chaos over a sick loved one. Sometimes though, the end is not positive. But even then, I am comforted by the knowledge that I did right by my patients; I did my damn best like I wish someone had done for my parents. But as a physician, you never let the negative emotions cloud your judgment. Emotionally, this is an easier burden to carry than stressing about things that I couldn't change. I have fought mediocrity all these years and have tried my hardest not to let my past define my future but after all these years, it still hurts that I help so many yet I couldn't help my own. That is my pager going off; I have another life to save.

ACKNOWLEDGMENT

To my mother, the giant on whose shoulders I stand; my father, whose sense of humor and wise counsel I still cherish; my siblings and aunt, whose love and support, I have enjoyed; the friends and all the strangers I've met on this journey, whose kindness and benevolence I will continue to cherish until I'm no more.

Dr. Shirley Ayuk-Takem, D.O

Dr. Shirley Ayuk-Takem, D.O is an ICU physician and philanthropist based out of the Houston, TX metro area. She is the CEO of Soleil Medical Group and completed her undergraduate studies at the University of Alabama in Birmingham, AL obtaining a BS degree in Respiratory Therapy. She worked for a few years as a Registered respiratory therapist and continued on to medical school at the School of Osteopathic Medicine in Arizona which is located in Mesa, AZ. She went on to do an Internal Medicine residency in Detroit, MI and a Critical care medicine fellowship in NJ. Having been educated and lived all over the US, she has a love of traveling and a passion for medicine and health care. Even though she typically sees critically ill patients, she tries to educate and instill health maintenance and disease prevention tips to her patients in an effort to keep them from coming back to the ICU. Additionally, she strives every day to bring compassion to her practice of medicine.

Dr. Raissa Fobi
Board Certified Pediatrician and Neonatologist

RUN INTO YOUR UNKNOWN

The Beginning.

On this rare day off, I find myself in a Palms Springs villa, celebrating a girlfriend's birthday. The sun warms my bare skin. The rest of my post-partum body is scantily clad in a size 14 bathing suit. Yes, you read that right: '**scantily clad**' and '**size 14**' in the same sentence. Mind over matter. The breeze rustles by quietly as I sit on the edge of the pool, with my feet lazily splashing in and out, enjoying the cool contrast the water provides.

My mind wanders as I sip an especially potent sangria, I concocted just moments ago. This safe space allows me the time and distance to consider the things that everyday life has me drowning out and ignoring. The phrase 'functional disability' comes to mind: a long-term limitation resulting from an injury, condition or illness. It is only when you are in a situation requiring you to use an ability or skill you thought you had, that you realize you lost it, as well as the magnitude and significance of what life has taken.

Last night, as part of the birthday celebrations, a group of us women went out, each beautiful and accomplished in her own right. While sitting at the bar I watched my friends dancing and talking with people so confidently, even though they just met. Aside from the people in my group, no one talked to me. Not even that awkward smile you exchange as you try to get a drink at the bar. They just turned their heads away. Such an insignificant thing really, but it was coming on the heels of major life changes, all of which had taken their invisible toll.

The most recent situation, and hence the one which informed my current state the most, was me splitting up with my fiancé, and him walking away from our eight-month old baby girl. Processing this emotional trauma, while working through brutally long shifts, had taken its toll. It was in essence, the straw that broke the camel's back. To me, in my sensitive emotional state, it translated to; *you are not beautiful.* **In big flashing neon lights**. The rational part of me knows that this had nothing to do with what I thought people saw, but more to do with my outside reflecting what I felt on the inside. It made me realize I did not feel confident, or attractive, or beautiful, or even seen. Just a few short years ago, I felt confident in who I was, and comfortable in my skin. The stark contrast between then and now, made me sad for what I had neglected to care for. Sad for what I eventually lost. It brought tears to my eyes as the realization dawned on me. **I had lost ME**!

I had worked hard to figure out who I was, and not only was I comfortable in, but I celebrated every aspect of myself: an African immigrant female physician who loves God, her family, food (#Ghana Or Gambian Jollof) and running. Oh, did I love running. And food. Can't decide which I love more. Imagine if you will, a 5'9", 190-pound woman, stumping away on the treadmill, with her thick 'em thighs rubbing away as she imagines the deliciousness of her next meal; that's me. But that is not the point. The point is, it took me a while to discover these things about myself. And many more years to nurture them, because self-care did not come to me naturally. In reality, having grown up in an African setting, it actually felt selfish.

In the Cameroonian home of my childhood, beyond keeping yourself clean and well groomed, the house clean and the daily meal prepared, the emphasis was on studying hard and caring for everyone around you. Even the career options your elders found acceptable had maximum earning potential, so that the baton of supporting the family could be passed on to you and your siblings. Or at least those of you who didn't flunk out of school. To prove my point, ask any African immigrant you meet what they do for work. The answer will be somewhere along the lines of engineer, accountant, lawyer, doctor or nurse. You're welcome. But I digress.

As my mother reminds me, I would grudgingly complain about being the one to care for this sibling or that cousin, while carrying out the task. But now that I have a daughter of my own, I have truly come to appreciate the value of this concept; It is a beautiful, warm and welcoming tradition that is necessary, but I think somewhat imbalanced. We grow up watching our mothers care for, and sometimes carry, their whole families. This auntie's daughter or the other friend's son. Stretching themselves and their resources thin, to make sure that the come-up is for everyone and not just their biological children. Pausing to relax, exercise, go for a massage, or getting their nails done was not a routine thing. Within this world, we women do not see self-care modeled. So, dissociating the guilt of spending this time and money on myself, from the act of carving out time to do something that brought me joy and built my insides, was a process.

Being blessed to live and work in America, surrounded by such a diverse population, most of whom embrace self-care as something as vital and natural as breathing, made that process easier. I discovered that my gateway to self-care was running. It gave me time to imagine the delicious foods I wanted to eat, yes, but also as important, to meditate and commune with God, plan my day or reflect on the things I was grateful for. On the treadmill, track or trail, I worked through the issues that I needed to resolve, all while getting my body moving to stay healthy and fit. After a long run, it always felt like my skin fit me just a tad bit better. I felt more capable of caring for my patients and my family. You should know though, that I have not always loved running. In fact, I came to it late in life. Thirty years late. I played tennis as a child, but by my teen years, I had dropped it. After that, I had a very spotty and tumultuous relationship with the gym. I am and have always been on the heavier side you see. Even at my leanest, I was 176-pounds. So, running did not always feel natural. But every time I got on the treadmill, I talked myself into holding on just long enough for the subjective feeling of torture to pass. It was a total of about five minutes. And after that, settling into a nice comfortable rhythm, felt like a leisurely drive on a sunny day, with the top down.

Besides being an African immigrant, I am a foreign medical graduate. My path to becoming a practicing neonatologist in this beautiful land of the free and brave, was not free and definitely did not feel brave. It felt necessary. Necessary to thrive. We had grown up watching our mother's generation doing the surviving. It was now up to us to move our families beyond that. *Beyond staying in relationships for the children's sake, to leaving said relationship to teach our daughters they deserve and can demand better. Beyond feeling guilty for buying that dress you love, to buying it because it brings you joy! Beyond saving your money for the inevitable emergency, to investing in growth opportunities to build generational wealth.*

It sounds cliché to say that I always knew that I wanted to be a physician. At the core of me, nothing else ever felt right. It was not a question of what I wanted to be when I grew up. It was, a question of how I take, this love in my heart, and pour it through my hands, so it helps a baby somewhere. The answer to my eight-year-old self seemed obvious, based on what I saw my mother do: become a

Doctor. So naturally, the excitement that came with my one acceptance letter out of twelve applications to medical schools in America, kept me up at night. My disappointment was equally as great, if not greater, when my parents told me they could not afford the cost of what it would take to send and keep me in medical school for a year. They had my siblings to consider as well. To a hormonal sixteen-year-old girl, that disappointment was immense. I laugh at my sixteen-year-old self because I only learned what true disappointment was, six months ago. But I am getting ahead of myself.

We started looking for alternatives to medical school in America, the most promising of which at the time, was South Africa. My journey in South Africa began in January of 1999, the year after affirmative action was introduced through the employment equality act, which in itself was only a mere four years after the end of Apartheid. The concept of racism had never really permeated my everyday life until then. Don't get me wrong, I know I am Black and African, but it is a concept that, before living in South Africa, did not trickle down into my every decision or thought. Before that, I was 'Ngebi'. After that, I was the black girl called 'Ngebi'.

It was a baptism by fire. So many instances of subtle and overt hatred, and anger. It was painful to learn how cruel people are to those they deem different. And the reactionary emotions these instances elicited from me, saddened me. Pure rage when a white, 6'3" 220-pound rugby player, physically assaulted and kicked me in the behind because I dared to be in a club that was known to be for white people only. Astonishment that a fellow black woman, who was an elderly Xhosa lady, followed my friends and I around the mall screaming 'Go back to your country'. Paralyzing frustration, when the genetics professor, who, in a class designated as English-taught, continued to lecture in Afrikaans with a smile on her face, even after I, the only black girl in her class of fifteen, asked her to switch to English because I did not understand. I learned to steel my nerves and persevere. I also learned to speak and write Afrikaans after that. Not that I am any good at it now, but the point is, I adapted to the circumstances before me. And throughout my three years in The University of Pretoria, South Africa (Go Tukkies!!), I still did not get into medical school.

Year after year I applied. Year after year I got rejected, because the quota for 'non-white' and 'foreigner' had been met: Three. The quota was three out of one hundred spots. Humbling, I know. For a brief moment, I considered giving up on pursuing medicine, and settling for less than what I knew I needed to become, in order to fulfill my purpose. But somehow, ignoring the persistent desire to try again, was a pill I just could not swallow.

So, I tried again. I applied only to and got accepted to the University of Ghana Medical school, in West Africa. Remembering my sixteen-year-old self's disappointment, I was hesitant to embark on the journey of higher education in America again. So, taking the United States Medical Licensing Exam (USMLE) was not a given. But that disappointment was not enough of a deterrent to keep me away from where I knew I had to go, in order to learn what I needed. So, I jumped back in and took the exam step that was congruent with the year of medical school that I was in at the time: Step 1. The rest of my time in medical school was a joyful monotonous drone of everyday, that was building to something bigger. I was content in my small corner of the world, drinking in all the knowledge I could, knowing I was working towards my ultimate purpose. The friends that eventually became family, joined my international village of fierce warriors, carving out their space in the world.

Somewhere in the middle.

After graduating from medical school, I ended up deciding to live and work in Ghana because, amongst other things, I had come to love the country so much. It became my short, mid, and long-term plan. For those two years, I rotated through the different departments of the Korle-Bu teaching hospital, working as a house officer, the lowest end of the totem pole. It's the equivalent of an intern, but without the cushy safety net of constant senior supervision and the fear of violating duty hours. There were just too many patients to see. You discussed the patients you saw with your supervising resident, at some point during the day. It felt like being thrown into a turbulent ocean with no floating equipment. The odds are definitely not in your favor, but I showed up to work every day excited and feeling like I was making a difference. In truth though, I was the one who was being changed. The four-year old who died because of a post liver biopsy hemorrhage, taught me how to sit with a family and offer my condolences with my presence, and not my words. The woman who had me running around the hospital at three in the morning, looking for just one unit of blood in any OR fridge, to save her life because she had just had her baby and was bleeding out, taught me to run for those who cannot walk. It also taught me to not accept '*the blood bank is out of blood*' statements of the world and go one step further for my patient. And, the elderly couple who smiled at me every week when they came to the breast cancer clinic for the wife's chemotherapy, taught me to find some measure of joy in the hardest of challenges.

You can see why I wanted to put the rest of the USMLE testing off. But my mother, would not let me stop there. She is a firm believer of the quote from Norman

Vincent Peale *"Shoot for the moon, even if you miss, you'll land among the stars"*. I had temporarily lost sight of what I always knew I wanted: to become a **Neonatologist**. I had become distracted with enjoying the feeling of no real accountability. My moon was still out there, and she knew it, so, after many encouraging phone calls from her end, in which she reminded me of some tough truths about life, I ended up taking my Step 2 clinical knowledge and skills tests.

This is me, having passed both exam steps, now ready to apply to pediatric residency programs. My applications numbered upward of forty. These different residency programs on the East Coast, by my research, were International Medical Graduate (IMG) friendly. So, it was appropriately shocking to me that I got only one interview offer. **ONE**. Let that sink in…**ONE**. My mother always says, *"Success is preparation meeting opportunity"*. I had prepared. I had just gotten an opportunity. A big opportunity at that. One could not have worked without the other.

For a breath of a second, I stupidly decided not to go to the interview because it was not on the list of my first ten choices. It seems so self-indulgent now. Bigger disappointments I guess make the smaller disappointments look their actual size. But at the time, I cried my silly tears, wiped them away, and went to the interview. The fear of not being good enough propelled me to prepare for that interview like I was going to meet President Obama. Sitting in the Department Chair secretary's office, waiting to be interviewed, the magnitude of the moment was not lost on me: I had not come this far only to come this far. I gave it everything I had.

The three months of waiting to hear if I got offered a position, were the most nerve-wracking of my life! So, when the offer of acceptance came, the tears that came with it were all happy ones. From an international student in an African medical school, to US licensing exams applications and interviews, it was an expensive process that totaled in the tens of thousands of dollars. On a Cameroonian physician's and architect's salaries, as the French say *"C'est pas évident"*. It wasn't always obvious where the funds would come from, but my parents kept borrowing from Peter to pay Paul just to make ends meet. And as you can imagine, they never let me forget it!

So, here I am, newly minted International medical grad, showing up for the first day of residency, in a crisp new white coat and excited for the journey ahead. Leaving my cocoon of familiarity in Ghana and moving to loud, bustling and dirty New York city, was exhilarating. Alicia keys had not exaggerated about it being a concrete jungle. The healthcare system in America was new and unknown territory to me. But I channeled the electric energy of the city, my determination to succeed and my excitement at finally being on the path to fulfilling my dreams, towards being worthy of the privilege to practice medicine, in the United States of America.

It was also during this time that I discovered the joys of running. In all of it, I was challenging myself to not accept less than what I knew I could give. And what a journey it was, with the ups and downs of any residency: the joys of the friendships made, the confidence gained from practicing evidence-based patient care, and the hunger for continued learning and growth. The recurring grain of sand in my shoe during this time though, was the struggle with what people's oversimplified idea of who *The Immigrant*, in this case *The African Immigrant* is. Our food is odorous yes, but this does not mean we smell. We all have thick accents, even though some of us, in an attempt to blend in, make ourselves sound more 'American'. This does not mean we don't understand

English, or that you have to slow down your speech for us to understand what you are saying. And to you fellow Africans, this does not also mean that we hate or are ashamed of our origins. You do what you think necessary to advance your position in life. If you do it for any other reason, that's your bowl of beans.

But the most vexing and the one I frequently encountered, is the insinuation that we are not smart or don't know enough about the subject matter to offer an informed and valid opinion. During a PICU rotation I was doing at an outside hospital, a fellow resident actually opened her mouth and let these words pass through what should have been the last barrier: *'Oh, you must be smart to have answered all the attending's questions'*. Yes, you heard me roll my eyes. No, Becky. Becky with the red hair in fact. Don't be like Becky. It was a dual process to navigate that one. You grow thicker skin so that these hurtful remarks don't penetrate and change your inner monologue. And at the same time, just like Aibileen from *The Help*, you play on repeat in your head *"You is kind, you is smart, you is important"*. But more importantly, you learn to not settle for what another person's narrative of you is. Little did I know that this would be a lesson that would serve me well in the future.

The resilience that comes from going through the circuitous route It took for my medical training, is what helped me in the darkest hours of my despair. I remember waking up on one of those cold February mornings this past winter and sitting on the edge of my bed. I groggily turned to look for my phone and saw the blood on my pillows. It had soaked through to the bottom. I touched my face wondering where all that blood had come from. My fingers land on my nose and I feel the crusted and dried blood. I had had a nose bleed as I slept. Judging by the amount of blood on my pillow, it had been a significant one. I don't have nose bleeds. A shiver ran down my spine as I wondered what would have happened if the bleeding had not stopped. Maybe all the stress from crying the night before, or the nonstop playback of the break-up argument in my head, or the eventual fitful night of sleep, had caused me to bleed. Whatever the reason, the mere thought of not waking up from my sleep and leaving my daughter with no parent who was there to care for her, shook me to my core. It was time to start picking up the pieces. I did not feel ready, but I had to start.

This part of my life has me hesitating to examine. Just like the scale in your bathroom that you see every day, you know you eventually have to dust it off and get on it at some point. I remember the acuteness of the pain all too well. Of my breakup that is, not the scale. Keep up people. The despair that the pain brought along, feels like they are just around the corner, right behind me. When it happened, I remember thinking that it probably was not a good idea to suggest that we continue dating, right after I had just told him the wedding was off and that I could no longer live with him. But I just was not ready to face the stark reality of being single, and a mom, just yet. Even as bad as things were, it was familiar. I had become comfortable in the drone of a less than mediocre life. Wash. Rinse. Repeat. It was easier to keep the unhealthy cycle going rather than stop, for fear that I could not pick myself up. And people depended on me to keep going. My daughter depended on me to keep going. My justification for this suggestion that we keep dating was that we would see a relationship therapist.

The reason we found ourselves at this point was because he had done it again. Big or small it always seemed to come back to this. To the fact that his choices and subsequent actions were always about him and not about what was good for our unit. I was tired of fighting, of quietly wanting better, of constantly being apprehensive of the next time. In the two years that we were together I went from a happy confident woman, to a woman who felt less than, in every way. A woman who had to ask to be held. I stopped running. Initially because of some pregnancy complications, but after the baby, I did not start back up because both my internal and external motivators were non-existent.

After this last fight I realized I could honestly not go back to the way things were. We sat at the table discussing our breakup like we were talking about the morning paper. I was just too tired and numb. I had been crying the whole night and did not sleep. We agreed to my suggestion that we keep dating while seeing a therapist. He goes upstairs to pack his things while I go online to look for said therapist. Fifteen minutes is all it took for my heart to break. In that space of time, he decided our working plan did not work for him, he booked and paid for his flight back home seeing as he had moved to this town for me. He reserved a hotel room where he would spend the nights prior to his flight. And he left the house. He walked away from his daughter. Without a hug, a kiss or even a second glance. My heart hurt for her. For the callousness with which he left her. For the questions she would grow up asking. There is no coming back from that in my book. It is over. No relationship therapist can fix deliberately walking away from my daughter.

There was an aspect of relief that I felt too. I could relax my internal fighting stance and re-direct that energy to building myself again. Beyond building myself, modeling for my daughter, what taking care of and valuing oneself looks like. I may not feel it just yet, but I damn sure will act like it, because she sees everything I do. So, I started with something that had proven effective in my life before: running. One step in front of the other, knowing that I would be sore in muscles I had completely forgotten about, I focused on the lightness my heart would feel as my feet picked up their pace on the treadmill. With tears running down my face, I ran my first mile in a year. And I have not stopped since.

Not the End.

So, here I am, a single mom. But it's a full circle sort of moment. That caring for everyone around you concept I grew up with, was my literal life saver. Family, friends, co-workers have rallied around me and continue to carry me through this. As a single physician mom, my life would literally not work without my mother being here, living with me, caring for me and her grand-daughter and watching her while I am away at work. Without, friends and in my case, the nurses I work with, offering their time and family members (probably unbeknownst to them), to help watch my daughter.

And I am away at work a lot. Mom guilt is a real thing. It's not going anywhere. So, it might as well pull up a chair and get comfortable. Single mom guilt though, does not want to sit by the fireplace with the rest of the things we beat ourselves up about. It is loud. Probably louder than the piercing shrieks my daughter cries only when I am walking out the door. My chest constricts as I imagine that her fourteen-month-old brain compares my walking out the door to her father walking out the door. But I have to walk out the door and go work. Emotionally dealing with it is a steep learning curve, and I am still on the gradient, so I have no advise on this one. Sorry.

I am dating again. Settle down, settle down! I should clarify, I am mom dating. It's so exciting! That moment when, as moms, your eyes meet and you size each other up, trying to decide whether the fact that your kids played well together in the ball pit is worth the awkwardness of starting a conversation and getting to know someone new, just for the potential of future play dates. The first couple of dates, will be under the guise of the kids getting together to play. But it will be an awkward dance of I'll show you mine if you show me yours: messy house, home projects, mom bods, losing weight plans, rowdy kids. Parenting styles. However, we are all still women, women with children. Women without children. Transgender women. Gay women. Younger women and older women. Married women and single women. And above all - women each with unique and valuable stories. Every woman should write a book. Every woman probably does write a book with her sighs, her tears, her choices and her lessons. This woman will leave you with the things my experiences have highlighted for me:

~ The first is that your past does not define your future, it only informs it, and only for as long as you let it. So, use it as a reference.

~ The different iterations of yourself are necessary. They require you to consciously participate in your growth.

~ You already know you can work hard, but you don't know how hard you can work until your life depends on it. Your life literally depends on your physical machine being in optimum operating condition aka becoming and staying healthy.

~ Run into your unknown. Whatever your gateway is into the discovery of you, use it. You may not know what you discover once you open that door, but, go ahead and open it. Walk, run, swim, dance, glide, prance, ride, pray, or meditate. Just move! But don't stay comfortable.

~ Nurture your villages people. Because like the African proverb says, *"When spider webs unite, they can tie up a lion"*.

~ Lastly, growth and hence, change will feel harder and more painful than it is. And just like labor, remember to breathe through it.

- Breath in as you prepare to work and push this painfully beautiful thing into existence, even if you cannot see its beauty just yet. Don't kid yourself, it will take active work. Prepare yourself.
- Hold your breath, stay consistent, keep pushing, don't stop working, because it is in consistency that you see results.
- Breathe out as you push past the last effort and you take stock of what you just accomplished or worked through.
- Do not dwell there to long though, lest you get too comfortable. Get ready to breathe again and push past your next achievement or challenge, great or small.

Stay pushing ladies, after all you were born inherently knowing how to do it.

ACKNOWLEDGEMENT

To my village of people near and far: May the Kola nut we share continue to hold us together.

Dr. Raissa Fobi

Raissa Ngebi Fobi, is a double board-certified Pediatrician and Neonatologist, and currently practices as an Attending Physician, as well as the Medical Director of the Neonatal ICU in Yakima Washington.

Dr Fobi was born in Yaounde Cameroon. She graduated from the University of Pretoria South Africa, with a Bachelor of Science focused in Human physiology and Genetics. She then went to the University of Ghana Medical school in west Africa, where she graduated with a Distinction in Anatomy. After graduating, she remained at the Korle-Bu teaching Hospital, where she worked for 2 years in a resource limited setting, caring for patients of all ages.

Dr Fobi immigrated to the United States in 2011, completed her Pediatric residency at The Columbia University affiliation at Harlem Hospital, and subsequently, her Neonatal-Perinatal medicine Fellowship at the University of California Irvine.

During her time in Fellowship training, her passion for the respiratory care of the premature newborn, naturally lead her to doing ground-breaking research, in the use of human Umbilical cord stem cell secretome and its role in ameliorating Bronchopulmonary Dysplasia. Alongside her mentor, she worked towards changing what is currently known about the treatment of this disease that premature newborns are significantly affected by.

Living in the pacific northwest, Dr Fobi loves being outdoors and is an avid runner. She also enjoys spending time with her family, her dog, and her spunky 13month old daughter Alia. Her approach to life is: Live simply, put love in action and be present in every moment.

Dr. Isabelle Mulango
Educational Commission for
Foreign Medical Graduates
Certified Physician

Dreams vs Reality

"No one is useless in this world who lightens the burdens of another."

~ Charles Dickens

I dislike the suspense of waiting and hospitals are by far the worst place for waiting. The seats are hard; they feel just too sterile, the buzz of machines disconcerting and the looming presence of fear palpable. Huddled together with my mother we sat in fearful silence and waited for what seemed like forever. Every now and then she listlessly paced around, stealing glances my way like I held the answers to all her unanswered questions. Well, don't look at me mother; this wait is killing me too.

Finally, the doctor came out a little disheveled and tired looking. I registered his grim face. The physician in me knew that could only spell one thing. His hesitation spoke volumes. But I needed to hear him say it. "Is she..." I croaked, too scared to even go on. I didn't need to finish though. He had done these enough times to know where I was headed. He quickly interjected and told me she would be alright. I guess the doctor's look reflective of one who had been subject to an insane workday and not one about to deliver some bad news. She had survived yet another scare and I was relieved to my core. She was being discharged.

Not too long after, she relapsed again with another acute illness. We remained hopeful, but then the call came. My pain was instant, squeezing my heart so strong and exploding my head with blinding whiteness. It made me dizzy. It made me reel and I could not hold back the seething torrent of tears. Not even the steady stream of liquid trickling down my face could cure the pain. I clutched my chest and staggered backward in my gait. I tried to breathe but each gasp tore down my throat and my mind raced even as I lost myself in the storm. No. My mentor couldn't be gone; not now when my life was just about to start. Not now when she could finally bask in glorious delight at her labor of love. Not now at all! The "I'm sorry" that followed choked the breath from my lungs and elicited a loud wail from my soul.

I was born during the rainy season in cold, wet Buea, Cameroon. It was August when the skies were tar black. Landslides were common and many villages were landlocked by the torrential rains. It was in these murky conditions that I made my dramatic entry into the world. My mother was in labor that unfortunately progressed to umbilical cord prolapse. In a panic, the frantic midwives sent for the only doctor available to the rural hospital while performing first aid measures in a desperate bid to keep mother and fetus alive. She only had to see the chaos in the delivery room to decipher that there was a need for quick action. She performed an emergency cesarean section, and mother and baby were okay once again. The baby was named after the nimble doctor. And like a prophet, she declared that the baby would be a doctor one day like her.

That doctor was Dr. Isabella Kahwah, and that baby was I, Dr. Isabelle Mulango.

*****

"A mentor is someone who allows you to see the hope inside yourself."
~ Oprah Winfrey

Baby Isabelle thrived; a chubby little bundle of smiles who morphed into an overtly inquisitive girl known for her ceaseless "why"; "but why". My childhood memories are filled with nights of noise, unrestrained laughter while playing cards and Ludo with my family and muffled tears when I did not win a game. My family lived in a small village in Buea, home to Mount Cameroon. Known for its volcanic activity and eruptions, I constantly witnessed the power of the mountain's tremor especially since our home was nettled right at the foot of the mountain. Particularly in the year 1999, our little, poorly constructed house will fracture in many corners during eruptions. We slept outside on such nights for fear of being buried under debris. In my child's eye, these were fun times! It felt like camping!

O yes, little Isabelle loved to play too. My days as a child were taken over by school and after games of hopscotch, double Dutch, single jump rope, "dodging" (a game with two people at opposite ends trying to shoot a player in the middle), dancing and climbing guava trees with the agility of a monkey. I would return home a sweaty mess; my dust-covered form bearing no resemblance to the clean child mother had bid goodbye to in the morning. Some days I would look so bad that I knew I was in for it should mother catch a glimpse of me. So, I would quietly sneak my dirty little self through the back door. Sometimes I was successful. Other times I was caught just before I completed my stealthy entry. I already knew the slash of the whip was coming next; not that the pain would deter me from skipping after school-play the next day. I was usually right back at it.

To curb my uncontrollable penchant for playing, my siblings enforced a routine of daily reading time. There was no escaping. Our home was always packed with relatives and I always was the youngest child. Hence, everyone tried to lead me on the right path and attempted to make me "Little Miss perfect". Therefore, there was always someone to implement my daily reading routine. We had no community library so their schoolbooks would do. Following a rocky start, I found out I loved reading and embraced the world of books with the same passion I had thrown into dirt tumbling. Reading birthed a wild and creative imagination, or perhaps it had always been in me but remained untapped while I rough-played in the mud and climbed trees for fun. I had no preference for what I read. Prose unearthed the storyteller in me; drama fueled the adrenaline rush and poetry- well poetry was lyrical. And so, I read on...

By age eleven, I had read: Eba's *"The Good Foot"*; Asong's *"Crown of Thorns"*; Achebe's *"Things Fall Apart"*; Bronte's *"Wuthering Heights"* and *"Jane Eyre"*; Dickens' *"Oliver Twist"*, *"Great Expectations"*, and *"Hard Times"*; Shakespeare's *"Twelfth Night"* and *"Julius Caesar"*; and Thiongo's *"The River Between"*; amongst others. What words I did not understand, I took to my siblings who got no rest till I was satisfied with the answer. They finally gifted me with a dictionary since they dared not complain. This path was their doing.

*****

"Education is the key to economic independence; do not give up for education is your first husband."
~ African Proverb

In school, I excelled. I had no choice because Mama wouldn't have it any other way. Mama had big dreams for her life which were not accomplished but continued to thrive in the lives of her children. Her favorite proverb for me was: "education is the key to economic independence, do not give up for education is your first husband". Like the former US First Lady Michele Obama said, "when girls are educated, their countries become stronger and more prosperous." Mama understood the power of girl child education, especially in underserved communities and did everything within her reach to make sure we were all educated.

But when it came time to head on to secondary school my mother was not able to cough up the 300,000FCFA ($600) yearly tuition needed to see me through boarding school. Unfortunately, life for us was a struggle as I saw my widowed mother doing several jobs. Her 8-5 job as a telecommunications technician and on weekends a subsistent farmer, petite trader, caterer, and cook. She never complained about putting on countless hats to feed and educate us. Not being able to afford to send me to boarding school was a devastating blow to my academic aspirations. Boarding schools were ranked in the top tier and it was the dream of every parent to offer their child that quality, albeit expensive education. But money was tight, and I had to make do with what Mama could afford- a day school some 30-minute walk away from home.

However, I was sick during the application period for schools and was taken to see Dr. Kahwah who had continued to be my pediatrician over the years. She asked about my studies and was visibly impressed by my performance in the final exams. When she asked what is next, we informed her I would go to the government day school come September, she was visibly appalled. "Preposterous!" she exclaimed. "Isabelle can't go to a day school. She is a candidate for boarding school". And right there she made a pledge partly to sponsor my education for the next seven years through secondary and high school. Wait, come again? Yes. Dr. Kahwah would be my sponsor and my mentor. This was getting even better. A few hours ago, I had been too weak to hold down my breakfast, but this news was enough to wipe out all traces of sickness from my person. I jumped in unbridled excitement like a new lottery winner. Well, I just received a seven-year uncontested grant, and I would study in a prestigious elitist educational institution. You can't tell me I couldn't beam, and you can't tell me Mama couldn't cry!

*****

"Never listen to anybody who tells you, you can't do it. You know you can so just get on with it." ~ Margaret Hirsch

I was admitted into Presbyterian Comprehensive Secondary School (PCSS) Buea where I completed the five years of my secondary school education before moving on to Presbyterian Secondary School (PSS) Mankon, Bamenda for high school. The lines kept falling for me in pleasant places. Within, two years into this new educational journey, I became the recipient of the Presbyterian Church in Cameroon (PCC) education award; a merit-based scholarship for academic excellence. This scholarship will fund part of my education for the next six years. At least now Mama wouldn't have to stress and struggle to come up with the rest of my tuition after Dr. Kahwah paid her part.

Boarding school was scheduled repetition: Up at 5:30 am, dash out to complete assigned housekeeping duties- sweeping, mopping floors, cleaning bathrooms, the refectory or the chapel- you did not get to choose. The mornings were brutal especially in a town known for its unusually cold weather. Showers were in open-spaced bathrooms and if you ever worried about being naked in front of twenty other girls, the freezing cold water quickly reminded you to do your thing and rush out if you wanted to make roll call at 6:30 am. Then there was morning devotion; the first of the religious activity you would be subject to in the day. Oh, and you had to sing the hymns too; the chaplain did not care if your voice was all hoarse from the bitterly frigid air outside. Another hymn; and sing again you must.

The routine was tough, but I did it with joy anyway. I was extremely happy at the opportunity of having a progressive education especially coming from humble beginnings. Boarding school honed my common sense, taught me good timekeeping, solidarity, patience, and faith while effortlessly finessing my quick wit and proclivity for learning.

*****

"For nothing will be impossible with God."
~ Luke 1:37

When it was time for university, the career options were a collective family discussion as the case in many African homes. I wanted Engineering but Mama said Medicine. These programs were only offered in select post-secondary institutions, and to secure entry, one had to take a highly competitive entrance exam. It was also a consensus that these exams were highly biased if only because most of the successful candidates hailed from the majority French regions, or came from influential families. The Engineering entrance exam came first but I would not get the chance to even test this theory. Mama exhausted all credit options but could not raise the money required to register me for the exam. Just like that, my dreams of becoming an Engineer were sadly buried. I wept!

By some miracle, Mama could raise the money needed for the medical school entrance. There were only three universities in the country that boasted of accredited medical programs; each admitting only about ninety students a year. Only one of these universities offered residency training. There was just enough money for me to register for all three entrance exams, so I did just that. I did not attend preparatory classes which most students took prior to sitting for the entrance exams; that was a luxury we could not afford. And so, I poured all of my heart, time and passion into self-study knowing that this could be the only chance I got at securing the future I wanted.

God must have wanted me to be a doctor; I tell you. Otherwise, how else could you explain the fact that I gained admission into all three programs without having any influential connections that would call in favors for me with the admissions committees? My only dilemma was choosing a medical school to spend the next seven years of my life. Ah! the problem of choice; the kind of problem I loved to have.

I chose the University of Buea because it was in my hometown. The language of instruction here too was English; unlike the other two institutions which were exclusively in French. However, we were yet to raise money for this new expensive journey and again I worried. Mama could not afford boarding school whose financial obligations paled compared to that of medical school. The cost of one medical textbook alone could feed my family for a few weeks. How would we make it? I took one day at a time with faith as my only companion.

*****

"Luck is what happens when preparation meets opportunity."~ Seneca

That summer holiday I did an observership at Dr. Kahwah's clinic. Even with tight finances, I still prepared for medical school. Dr. Kahwah was floored when she heard of my outstanding results and like that day, seven years ago, she made another pledge. She would sponsor my tuition for my first year in medical school!

I was now mature enough to appreciate the magnitude of benevolence this woman was selflessly extending yet again like one bursting at the seams with inexhaustible wealth. She wasn't filthy rich, but she was kind and a true mentor; a recurring realization which made me cry in humble appreciation.

The first few days on the university campus were surreal. It was my first time in day school and navigating early adulthood. The campus was also way larger than what I was used to. The curriculum was another story altogether. This was the big brother to the advanced biology we did in high school; the chemistry belonged to an advanced science lab, and the physics felt like we were being prepared to rebut all of Einstein's theories. And not only did I have to worry about digesting all the complex names and concepts I was now being introduced to, I still had to worry about funding for the next 6 years.

I tried my luck at the PCC scholarship again and I was selected. I was awarded funding for the next three years which was a welcomed respite again for my family. I could now freely lose myself into the program of study which got more interesting with every passing day. Meanwhile, my mother continued working tirelessly day and night to cover other related medical school expenses.

When graduation day came, mother was the beaming picture of maternal pride. Isn't it said that the best mothers raise the best physicians? Dr. Kahwah was there too; ever-supportive and contagiously happy on my newest accomplishment. At just 25 years old, this degree was as much her handiwork as it was mine. Family and friends were plenty too. It was a very well-deserved victory for all of them. It takes a village to raise a child, they say, and I couldn't agree more. It took them all to raise me.

*****

"Be courageous and don't ever give up an opportunity to do better. Mentor another girl."~ Dr. Isabella Kahwah

My first job came, and I was a General Practitioner (GP) in the very hospital I had been born in. Look at God! It was deeply satisfying and humbled to serve my own people and offer a healing touch to the hands which had once carried me when I was too little to remember or comforted a fall when I was too rambunctious to know better. It should have been a time of unmatched bliss for me, but it wasn't. Dr. Kahwah was getting very sick and called me for a second opinion. It was strange, this role reversal where now she was the patient and me, the physician. And much like a child who likes to believe in the infallibility of a parent, the mentee was now the mentor, I was very humbled.

But she did. She was very proud to see the chubby baby she delivered and mentored, now giving her informed medical opinions. She was a feminist; a strong proponent of the education of the girl child and the emancipation of the voiceless women. In my last in-depth conversation with her, she reminded me as she always did: *"be courageous and don't ever give up an opportunity to do better. Mentor another girl."* Iconic words from an iconic woman gone much too soon.

The pain I felt at Dr. Kahwah's passing was profound especially because I felt like I didn't get a chance to give back to her. I still hurt when I remember her. She helped make me who I am today. Every day is hard as I try to move on and continue her legacy by paying it forward.

*****

"Success is not final; failure is not fatal: It is the courage to continue that counts."~ Winston S. Churchill

It is past 3 a.m. in the emergency room (ER) of a rural hospital in Cameroon and calmness has taken over after an eventful and adrenaline-rushed day. The night had been filled with emergencies including a toddler with severe malaria and malnutrition needing an urgent blood transfusion. The patient's mother had traveled on a motorbike from a nearby village to seek medical treatment at our facility; the only one within traveling distance from her residence. She was desperate and frantic; like any mother with a sick child would be. She was in luck; this time was unlike many others, we had a full running blood bank today; her child would be fine. One room away was another young woman referred from a traditional birth attendant for a breech delivery. She was triaged and we had performed an emergency cesarean section. There were a few minor wound lacerations repairs done following motor vehicle accidents; a broken head from a drunken fight we had to stitch earlier on. It was his third visit here in three months for the same reason. I hope he didn't grace us with a fourth. Yes, it was a typical day at the ER.

Things were finally dying down and I seized the opportunity to check my email. I had been longing to do so all evening. I inserted the feeble bandwidth internet key to my laptop. My heart is pounding with fear and many questions. I am now a click away to the United States Medical Licensing Examination (USMLE) Step 1 results that I had taken a couple of months ago in the United States (US). This will change everything for me. In this still moment, I nursed the courage to read the email from the Educational Commission for Foreign Medical Graduates (ECFMG). Their news was enough to shatter whatever iota of peace the day had given. I failed! I, the straight-A student of secondary and high school; I, the repeat meritorious scholarship recipient; I, the triple admitted medical school applicant; I, the doctor already earning peer recognition in the short time of practice; I, the one who had been mentored by one of the best in the field...failed an exam. It was shocking and deeply painful. I thought about all the sacrifices my family and I had made for my trip to and from the US to take this exam and I thought about the long hours of study I had to put in after work when all my tired body wanted was sleep. I desperately wanted to cry but my tears failed me. As much as I loved my patients, I desperately prayed that no one would set foot into the ER until my shift ended at 6 am. I needed this alone time to wallow in my pain and lick my wounds of defeat.

I was certain Dr. Kahwah was turning over in her grave. Then the self-doubt started creeping in. Feelings of unworthiness overwhelmed me. Was I even deserving of her extreme kindness? Over 1000 reasons flickered through my mind as to why I "shouldn't have", attempting to convince myself that by failing this exam, our sacrifices had been misdirected and wasted.

As soon as the first physician showed up at 6 am, I hopped on the first available motorbike for the 15-minute ride to my apartment. This time the tears had finally come, and I cried unabashedly. My tears pouring down in rivulets faster than the early morning breeze could dry. I didn't even have a safety helmet on, and I didn't care. In my grief, I questioned my purpose and pondered if traveling abroad to pursue a career in medicine was a necessary feat.

*****

"Failure is simply the opportunity to begin again this time more intelligently." ~ Henry Ford

After a grieving period, I had to harness optimism and refocus my thinking. The next few months were challenging. I had to manage a career as a young general physician practicing in a district hospital, raise funds for the next trip to the US and exam preparation materials/fees for the subsequent exam season. It was also a time of deep soul searching and questions. In times of disappointments do you cry and wail or assess the root of the problem? Who do you reach out to for guidance? I let these fundamental questions shape my thoughts as I contemplated my next plan of action.

I would draw inspiration from my mother Joan Mulango, the woman who was once a young girl with big dreams of becoming a physician but was forced to chart a new path when life happened. My mother often told me the story of a young Malawian Legson Kayira in his autobiographical novel "I Will Try" which she learned as a teenager in form three (tenth grade) literature class in 1971. He had left his homeland as a teenager to pursue an education in America. Much like Kayira, my mother was the daughter of poor farmers. The fourth of nine children, her chance at a prized education was sacrificed at the altar of her brothers'- her father gave priority to his sons when economic hardship forced some of his children out of school. Yet she persisted; working in her father's cocoa farms, cleaning yards, and climbing palm trees to raise the money to fund her secondary school education. The year her father died she would stay out of school for a whole year trying to raise fees for form four (eleventh grade) education. Her quest for education was unrelenting. Years later she completed high school, got married and became a young widow with five children. Yet she was the matriarch of her family; taking over the care of her vast extended family with little complain as she battled multiple jobs.

I also remembered my benefactor, Dr. Kahwah and motivation started creeping in. For someone to sacrifice her hard-earned finances to support me was mind-blowing. Even more amazing was the fact that giving to me seemed to have been a great source of joy for her as she celebrated my triumphs and stood by me in times of distress. How then, could I return her generosity and affection especially now that she had moved on to the great beyond. How else could I indeed payback when I couldn't, even though I wanted to?

As I reflected on my mother's life story and Dr. Kahwah's generosity, I quickly realized that to focus on my feelings of unworthiness would be to dishonor their sacrifices and the beautiful spirit in which it was so lovingly given. I knew giving up was not an option. I would try again.

*****

"Keep trying till you get it right."
~ Malingo Elangwe

After my first unsuccessful attempt at the USMLE Step 1, I continued working as a GP gathering experience, providing care to underserved populations while still studying for American licensure. I made multiple trips to the US to take the USMLE step 1 and 2 Clinical Knowledge (CK) and Clinical Skills (CS) and I passed after several attempts. Every time I considered quitting, I remembered that someone else did not give up on me and forged on. My beloved aunt, Malingo Elangwe always told me, "Keep trying till you get it right". That has remained my mantra till this day.

*****

"Service to others is the rent you pay for your room here on earth." ~ Muhammad Ali

My life so far has taught me much about giving. As a young girl, I watched my mother share her very last dime even though she herself couldn't boast of much. Ours was the house where everyone knew they would be guaranteed a warm meal or a place to rest. As long as there was food, clothing, and shelter for us, mother would share the little extra she had with the next person. The older I got, the more I got to agree with her. There is such a sense of fulfillment that comes with serving that the only regret I have is that I didn't start sooner.

Learning by example, I have tried to do my share of service as a Physician. I spend every free time I get galloping muddy terrains to get to the next remote village to offer free health screenings and consultations. While I can never repay the kindness that was shown to me, the only way I know I can come close is by paying it forward. My mother and Dr. Kahwah were the wind beneath my wings and I understand that to appreciate the gift of giving, we too have to become givers. By engaging wholeheartedly in giving, we create exponential possibilities from single acts of kindness. Do not worry about the size of your gift. Dr. Kahwah did not pay my entire tuition, but the portion she paid was just enough. Do not say the need is too great. You don't have to give it all. Just give the little you have.

Most often, people and even our own ego step in to make us feel like we are a charity case. You hear yourself saying to your giver, "O no, you don't have to," even when you know you desperately need their gift. Other times, we simply felt unworthy of kindness. Do not allow these untruths to poison the beauty of kindness. Instead, allow yourself a moment of grace, and remember your giver is challenging you to acknowledge your own worth as seen through their eyes. Therefore, rather than shy away from kindness say, "Thank you" and pay it forward.

*****

"You are today where your thoughts have brought you. You will be tomorrow where your thoughts take you."

~ James Allen.

For me, the journey to US residency continues and the next time you will likely read something from me will be about my transition in the US and life in residency! It has been a long tedious road shaped by benevolence and destiny. I have learned to celebrate the little accomplishments as much as I celebrate the great, refusing to let setbacks bring me down.

My word of advice? Be authentic; your story, history all brought you to this moment and there is a reason for that. Be mindful. Any act of kindness, regardless of its size, has the potential to change not only the partakers but all those around them. Be purposeful. On dark days, surround yourself with positive influencers who are committed to helping you grow and living your dreams. Ultimately be positive. Think it, believe it and with a little help, you will achieve it. In the words of James Allen, *"you are today where your thoughts have brought you. You will be tomorrow where your thoughts take you."* And while you are at it remember to be kind. Not only to others but also to yourself.

ACKNOWLEDGEMENT

To my mother, family and all the phenomenal women who raised me especially Malingo.

Dr. Isabelle Mulango

Dr. Isabelle Mulango earned her MD at the University of Buea, Cameroon in 2014. Her very first duty station as a General Practitioner was a rural hospital where she provided comprehensive care and consultations to children and adults in an inpatient, outpatient, and emergency department setting. She has hands-on clinical experience in primary care and has served as coordinator for Diabetes & Hypertension and HIV/AIDS committees.

Born and raised in Cameroon, Dr. Mulango grew up in a country with significant health workforce shortage which helped her develop an interest in promoting health literacy and bridging the gaps in healthcare delivery. In addition, she is a die-hard advocate for the integration of mental health services in primary healthcare.

Dr. Mulango loves volunteering and oftentimes provides free medical services in underserved areas and orphanages, organizing workshops to educate women and girls on thermal issues, and mentoring young girls to study STEM programs in Cameroon.

She is ECFMG certified and is currently pursuing US clinical experience for residency in psychiatry and/or family medicine. Dr. Mulango is also the co-author of the inspiring book – *Beyond Challenges*, which narrates the hurdles faced by African immigrant women, in relation to life, love and the practice of medicine in the United States. Aside from being a physician, Isabelle enjoys music, cooking and traveling to explore new cultures.

Dr. Clarisse Tallah
Family Medicine Physician in A Maternity Care Fellowship

Didn't See it Coming

The call came in on Wednesday, May 2013 at exactly 10:45 p.m. Until that moment, the humdrum of daily life carried on in our hillside apartment in Grand Anse, St. George, Grenada. A cool gentle breeze whistled softly in the silent night muggy air, interrupted by chirping crickets and the occasional barking of our Landlord's dogs as strangers' strode past our gate. My roommate, Stacy, answered on the third ring. While it was normal to hear from her 'study buddy', Jessie, the nature of the call was anything but. With no explanation, Jessie urged her to meet Jackson at the apartment gate in 15 minutes. Almost as an afterthought, just before hanging up, Jessie added, '... bring Clarisse as well'. Not being particularly close to either Jessie or Jackson like Stacy, hesitation and discomfort were my overriding sentiments. But we both agreed it was strange that whatever it was had to be addressed at 11pm at night given we were all busy studying for our medical school exams.

Prepared to be a third wheel, I donned a sweater and threw on sandals. We made our way to the gate at the sound of Jackson's vehicle trudging up the hill. The dogs barked incessantly as we opened up the gate and waited for Jackson to park and alight from his vehicle. Operating on high anticipation and little patience, it took a lot not to scream at him to walk a little quicker. Still, something was off about his demeanor. His sober countenance should have been an indication of bad news. It was easy, however, to chuck his serious expression up to stress and the rigors of studying for upcoming exams. After a brisk greeting, in one sentence, he slowly and deliberately delivered the news about Nyanjera. My knees immediately felt weak and threatened to buckle as

I leaned on the gate behind me for support. Glancing over in Stacy's direction, her hands were clasped over her mouth as she took a step backward, wide eyed in disbelief. With a sting of tears, we returned our gaze to Jackson who further explained the details of the news. Being Nyanjera's former roommates, Jackson had insisted on delivering this news in person in an attempt to soften the impact of the blow. The unacceptable alternative was learning the news from the local newspapers the next day. He then paused in a deliberate attempt to allow the news to register given the puzzled stares on our faces. Jackson then chivalrously offered to take us to Jessie's apartment where other classmates had gathered.

Coming out of what felt like a trance, we declined his offer and thanked him. We said our good nights as we closed the gate and walked back to the apartment in silence. Studying ended prematurely for the night. Instead, we sat in the living room and stared at the walls lost in deep thought. We racked our brains for the next three hours trying to decipher our new circumstances and its implications. Once in bed, I felt a level of moral culpability. How did I not see this coming? Would the circumstances be different if I had intervened? I sighed and flipped my pillow which was now soaked with tears as I perseverate on every detail of Jackson's news.

Entry into a U.S. medical school could be extremely challenging for an immigrant. You were either a genius or had great networking abilities if you succeeded. Given I fell into neither category, as Cameroonian, I opted for education at an international medical school. First in the United Kingdom (U.K.), in a Global Scholar Program August 2011, followed by a second year in Grenada. On the first day of medical school in the U.K., I met Stacy and Nyanjera.

We were assigned a flat with 3 other roommates that first year of medical school. With six different personalities living in the same space, we were obliged to make it work. Given how neat and tidy we were, we bonded over the flat upkeep to prevent the pig sty we had witnessed in other flats. The curriculum kept us in sync. Classes began at 7am prior to sunrise. We left the study hall after 5pm at sunset. Everything was new and different at New Castle Upon Tyne, from the culture, temperature, to the academic demands.

Being a native English speaker, it was baffling that I struggled to comprehend the Geordie accents. I asked for three to five slow repetitions to fully grasp the message. Challenged to find palatable food, I quickly settled for a deep fried chicken joint, friendly to my student budget. Moving from Atlanta, Georgia, this new weather felt like Antarctica, always cold and dark all year round. Bundled in multiple layers all year, we rejoiced during a one week long spring-like weather in June. School-wise, I had transitioned from college with bite size amounts of information, long study periods for material assimilation and effortless excellent grades to the complete opposite. It felt like a 5000 page textbook size material every week, no time for assimilation and mediocre grades despite putting in a threefold effort. We looked forward to most weekends, not for a break, but to attempt to catch up with lagging material. All weekends were spent with Cindy, my study buddy for 12 hours straight. We allowed a thirty minute to an hour lunch break, otherwise we spent the whole day deciphering the medical literature of the week and quizzing each other.

Stacy, Nyanjera and I bonded over the brutality of medical school compared to our college years. Once after convincing Nyanjera to style my hair, we had an in depth conversation about being African and female in America. It included our passion and drive in the pursuit of a healthcare profession. Nyanjera was from Kenya, another African country like myself. So of all classmates, she understood the challenges of an 'Alien' immigration struggle. We agreed on the dislike of the immigration term 'Alien' which implied we the immigrants, are from out of space. I shared my insecurities about success in medical school, fearing I might flunk out given how challenging it was. The grade transition was from mostly A's with occasional B's to now B's to C's and seldom A's. My new realization was a hard pill to swallow.

My family had sacrificed a limb to get me here. So I cringed thinking of how disappointed they would be if I failed. Frustrated and desperate for inspiration, I called my mother two weeks prior, short of breath from crying over the mediocre mid-term grades. In one particular class, I was sitting on the fence of pass/fail with only one more exam to go. My mom had laughed in her usual calm way. Reassured there was nothing more serious going on, she remarked '...medical doctor or not, I will always love you'.

I slept well after that. Nyanjera who had been patiently and quietly absorbing my melodramatic vent, erupted into a loud laugh followed by a sigh. "I can relate… But Clarisse, you should have more faith in yourself'. 'We have already defied the odds thus far for even making it into medical school', she explained. 'You can't get caught up on grades just be a kind and compassionate physician'. Patients could not distinguish the A scoring physicians from the rest. They could however tell a good one from a bad one. She spoke with conviction and assertiveness as she dissected each of my emotional queries and paired them with a corresponding psychological solution. It was admirable and therefore it didn't come as a surprise when Nyanjera announced she wanted to be a psychiatrist. She felt the burden of the stigma surrounding mental health and the under treatment and wanted to circumvent it. Nyanjera and myself also bonded over our 'absentee' Dads. Nyanjera's Dad left her Mom when she was very young, whereas mine was physically present but emotionally absent. We playfully debated over which situation was better and jointly concluded my situation was better. I could see a hint of sadness in her eyes as she briefly elaborated on her father. I decided not to push for details in fear of causing more pain.

Nyanjera was quiet, timid and always looked effortlessly beautiful. She had a heart of gold. She enjoyed a smoke of cigarettes ever so often. Privacy was essential for her. She mostly kept to herself, so I respected her privacy despite craving more of her company. For instance, we would exchange texts asking to borrow sugar, flour e.t.c. instead of asking in person. After all, we shared a wall in our flat. She once hand made a thank you card after I offered her a band aid for one of those annoying cuts from shaving. Nyanjera always came through for you when you needed her. She was always calm in the face of a storm and always seemed to know how to navigate obstacles. Before the end of the first year of medical school, Nyanjera announced she was seeing Sam and seemed happy, so I thought.

Having survived that first year, the next year we moved to Grenada for our second year of medical school. Scarred by living with five flat mates with varying hygiene preferences, Nyanjera opted for a one bedroom apartment. Stacy and I rented a 2 bedroom apartment about one mile from Nyanjera's apartment. In addition, our classroom size increased from 50 to almost 200 students. That meant I saw Nyanjera seldom. I would see her occasionally in and around the classroom. She was not in my small study groups either, which was determined by first letter of last names. We would try to catch up by grabbing lunch together while chit-chatting. Conversations ranged from criticism of material presentation of certain professors, superficial updates on family events or recent developments on Sam. Nyanjera would giggle when referring to Sam. I teased her about having ''butterflies in the stomach' and wished her well. Nyanjera and Sam could be spotted from time to time walking back home together. However, they did not formally attend events together or introduce each other as their significant others. I doubt many people knew they were dating. Again, privacy was always Nyanjera's preference.

Meanwhile, school got even harder. This year we studied subject courses such as Pathology and Physiology which were arguably two of the most grueling courses in medical school. This semester was no different from the previous. Our lives still revolved around studying, eating and sleeping. Lectures began around 7 - 8am where as usual voluminous amounts of material were thrown our way. This was followed by a lunch break after which we broke up into small groups and presented our pathology slides individually. We concluded small group studies around 6:30pm followed by dinner. You then rushed home to work on preparing slides for the next day which typically took anywhere from two to three hours. You had to then review material from the day in order to complete any other homework. You were grateful to make it to bed by 1:30am.

To my utter dismay, things started to take a turn for the worst. There were strange and scary back-to-back events. It began with my iPad, which at the time was a big deal, but in hindsight became the least of my worries. As though things were not stressful enough, my iPad with a considerable amount of medical school notes and homework got stolen.

Preoccupied by the tasks ahead of me, I had absentmindedly walked out of the gym forgetting to retrieve it by the weights. While on the bus headed home from school campus, I reached into my bag on the third stop. When it became evident it wasn't in its usual location, I began ferreting around my book bag. Immediately, I felt a rush of heat throughout my body and my heart rate sped up upon the realization that l had no recollection of grabbing it from the floor. There was a five-hour homework project I had completed and saved in my iPad. This project was due the next day in the afternoon. Of course that had to be the period during which my MacBook Pro had conveniently stopped working 2 weeks prior. It was shipped to an Apple Store in the United States for repair and was not due for another 1 month.

I was dependent on my iPad and the library computers. I bolted out of my seat as though my seat had become uncomfortable hot and briskly walked towards the front of the bus. Once at the front, I pleaded with the driver to let me out of the bus immediately. In response, he shut me an irate look and refused to stop the vehicle at a non-designated bus stop. He eventually caved at my insistence and let me out. l got out apologetic and thanking him. I ran the whole one mile back to the school gym. Feeling my chest beginning to tighten up from an asthma flare under the hot sun, I pressed on, fearing slowing down will ensure my iPad got stolen. Drenched in sweat and trying to catch my breath, I immediately went to the weights, but it was too late, my iPad was gone. I looked around the gym, stopped at Lost and Found, and asked some students at the gym, but no one agreed to have seen it. Walking away in a share state of panic, I switched to 'damage control' mode going over how to recreate my homework. Later that night, I tried 'Find my iPad' feature to no avail, so I opted for 'lost' mode setting instead. I figured if the iPad could not be used, eventually it would be abandoned.

Feeling beaten up and livid at my stupidity, I took the next available bus headed home as I pondered my strategy for recreating my homework on time without compromising sleep. Then, there was a sudden loud 'bang', interrupting my thoughts and quickly forcing me back to reality. The impact caused me to come flying off my seat. Luckily, my fall was halted by the seat ahead, banging my knee caps. I looked up frightened but grateful that I had not occupied the usual seat on the first row right behind the driver. Seating in that position would have ensured that I came off my seat flying towards the wind shield. The front of our bus was flushed against the back of another vehicle about 4 times smaller. The bus driver immediately jumped out the bus to check on the driver and passengers in the vehicle ahead. Luckily no one got hurt in either vehicle. The only sign of collision was an askew rear bumper. The drivers exchanged insurance information and we continued on our way.

Being from an African heritage full of superstitious and deep religious beliefs, I couldn't help but ponder what all of this meant. Were these two events warning signs for worse things to come or a sign to slow down? Three weeks later after three hours spent re-creating the home work and almost 10 hours towards note recuperation, my iPad was eventually recovered by the campus security and returned.

We have a saying in Cameroon that is predictive of a good outcome when experiencing worsening back to back challenges. It goes, 'When it rains, it pours'. This is to imply when faced with challenges, they would get worse before getting better. The next major event that second year of medical school was the passing of my Father. It was yet another automated day of class, studies etc when I noticed six missed calls from my Uncle. Transitioning from one scholarly activity to another, I ignored his calls postponing a return call back for the evening. That night, I came to understand why my uncle had been calling incessantly.

While studying, my brother called and stated, "The phone call we have all been waiting for finally arrived". My father who had been battling illness for several years had quickly and drastically deteriorated within a few weeks. He had finally succumbed to the disease. My initial reaction was denial followed by anger as the news sank in. Why had I been dealt this card in life? How could my father of all people be dead? I broke the news to Stacy with tears streaming down my face. Stacy cried with me as she tried to console me. If emotional distress could be weighed in pounds, I felt an added 300 pounds of burden in addition to the extra 50lbs representing school stressors that was usually. All I could think of was how I needed a break from all of my stressors. This was an excessive emotional burden that was beyond my ability to process. Given the geographical distance from home, my mother had spared me the details surrounding his death. With a full knowledge of my current situation, she wanted to prevent additional emotional stress and turmoil.

Consequently, even though I knew he was very sick, I had not processed the gravity of his illness to realize it was dire. I went to bed that night, hoping this was all just a horrible dream. The next morning, after having several vivid dreams about my father, the following thought crossed my mind, "Daddy would want me to keep going". It was also during this time that I drew on my faith for encouragement with yet another overused Cameroonian phrase: 'God does not give you anything you can't handle'. This was my cross to carry and I planned on doing it non grudgingly.

This self motivational talk didn't last long. With this new found strength, I went through the motions of my usual daily rituals, doing what I needed to do to stay afloat. However, irrespective of what I did, my mind constantly drifted to the circumstances surrounding his death. There were random unprovoked spurts of tear outbursts, which caused my peers to worry about me. During this period, I began experiencing a damp on the flames that provided my fiery pursuit of medicine. For the first time in my brief medical career, I was well adapted to the rigor of medical school and was doing well in all of my classes. What timing! After obtaining an absentee permit from school plus financial help from my brother, I boarding a plane to Cameroon for my father's burial.

The raw pain and emotion did not surface till I arrived at the gate of my childhood house in Yaounde, Cameroon. That evening was the 'wake keeping', implying there were just under 200 well wishers at the house. They were singing religious hymns while dancing, interspersed by prayer to celebrate my father's life. As to be expected in the Cameroonian culture, my father's remains would be at home for viewing. This was customary that the dead had to be brought back to their home one more time for a proper and last farewell. The tears started freely flowing as I ascended up our steep hill leading up to my house. Looking to my right, the gated pool was open and all around was a sea of people. There were more people on the driveway and in the house. Blinded by my own tears, I couldn't make out the faces but was appreciative and at the same time overwhelmed by all the love and support. The first well wisher to embrace me was my beloved primary school teacher, who had taught me how to read and write. He had also blossomed by book worm habits and my amplitude for listening and telling stories. At the corner of my eye, I spotted an adorned mahogany coffin through the clear doors of the living room. Words cannot describe the feelings that followed. It almost felt like an out of body experience as I stood there in a trance. My heart immediately began racing as though I had completed a one mile sprint. This was closely followed by diffuse and profuse generalized diaphoresis. 'Daddy is really dead', I thought to myself. At that point, I intended to turn around and run away from there, as though running away will undo my father's death and lift the overwhelming sorrow and heartbreak. Sensing my heightened emotional turmoil, my brother who had led me up the house from the gate, tightened his grasp on my hand. Glancing at me, he led me through the back of the house as though reading my mind. In the kitchen I fell into a tight embrace first with my mom and then my sister still crying uncontrollably.

My mother gently asked if I was ready to see my father, I shook my head. So instead, she led me upstairs to my father's former room. Here I cried for another couple of minutes while processing my new reality that my father was gone forever. When I was ready, we came down for a mass service in the front yard. Two hours later, upon the conclusion of mass, it came time to view the corpse. Gingerly approaching my father's coffin in the living room, he slowly came into full view. I saw a cachectic man, much darker in complexion and covered from the waist down by the bottom half of the coffin door. He was dressed in a black suit, a black bow tie tied around the neck of a pristine white shirt, and wore white gloves with his hands stacked on each other. He had a cross placed on his chest plus a white beautiful rose sticking out of his breast pocket. His illness had ravaged him making it seem like the man in the coffin was only my father's look- alike. Reaching out a hand to touch him, I suddenly heard an animal-like scream followed by an ugly and angry cry. It took me a full second to realize it was coming from me. I had always thought my father was invincible. But here he was, motionless in a box never to be seen or heard from again. A kind of cold 'numbness' descended on me at my near realization. I knew I would never be whole again.

We buried him in Nso, the village in which he was born and raised. Same day after the burial, I immediately started my trip to return to school. This was delayed by two days due to the Sandy hurricane leading to two flight cancelations. While in school, I took all three exams I had missed within four days of arrival. Somehow I managed not only to pass, but to supersede the class averages. This came as a surprise because I barely studied for these exams given the circumstances. It then dawned on me that my father was now probably taking care of me in ways he could not have while he was alive.

Now back from Cameroon, more and more I lacked interest in school work. I understood this was transient and I had to keep going, if not for myself, then to honor my father's wishes and sacrifices. Like a typical African father who came from humble beginnings and later became financially equipped, he sent all three of his children to the United States in hopes of a better life. My lack of interest in school work then spilled over to almost everything in life. I had a hard time concentrating in class and my grades had started to slowly reflect my poor focus.

Slowly, I became introverted as I know mostly preferred studying on my own without Cindy who I literally did all studying with prior to the burial. This was highly unusual for me. Sleep was not restful and eating became a chore. My friends sensed these changes and kept reaching out to me for support. Unintentionally, I pushed them away, avoiding them and lying to them with my automated response, 'I am doing great'. Reaching out to the one place I typically drew strength from, only gave more anguish. My siblings and Mom were also going through the same emotional struggles which manifested as high tensions and unfortunately conflict amongst us. We distanced each other, retreating to our emotional respective corners to lick our wounds in isolation. I knew something was wrong but I couldn't quite put a finger on it. It was highly unusual that I did not feel like myself and was losing control over my life. This is when I chose to seek help and talk to Mr. Thomas. He was the medical school counselor and should be able to help me figure out how to improve my school grades. He probed and within 20 to 30 minutes he made the correlation of my life stressors and my academics. Mr. Thomas concluded that I might be suffering from the onset of clinical depression due to my father's death and lack of social support. He recommended I exercised more consistently and to consider antidepressants if there was no relief.

Coming from a place like Cameroon where mental health is poorly understood and highly stigmatized, I was shocked at this new revelation and to be honest, felt insulted. The Clarisse Tallah I knew was a cheerful person. Was there a chance Mr. Thomas was mistaken? In my naivety, I laughed off Mr. Thomas comments and then set out to prove him wrong. The next day, I decided I would become happy again at all cost. Even though skeptical, I grudgingly heeded

Mr. Thomas advice and started jogging every day. This gradually improved by mood. I then joined a Bollywood dance group and even choreographed a routine for my dance group. We performed at our end of year talent show and won first place. I gradually gained control of my life once more. Years later, I now realize Mr. Thomas was right on point, I screamed depression in my actions. I am happy I chose to seek help and paid attention to his advice.

I had a conversation with Nyanjera about this whole situation and how I had been labeled 'depressed'. Being ever supportive, she responded, 'Clarisse we are both going to work out and get you out of this funk'. She disclosed she was stressed out about 'family stuff' and was going through 'alot' but would not elaborate further. During this period, we went to the gym together and worked hard with a personal trainer. Exercise meet-ups were early on most days, lasted an hour and a half and occurred every other day. Nyanjera was inspirational. She was strong, energetic and very fit. I on the other hand was completely opposite, and could barely keep up, forcing the trainer to provide exercise modifications. She kept up with all vigorous exercises thrown our way, egging me on as I struggled to keep up. With her encouragement I slowly built endurance and was fully able to execute the exercises. Before we knew, school was in recess and I went home with decent grades thanks to prayer, great friends, dance classes and my exercise sessions with Nyanjera.

I returned to my last semester of school in Grenada Jan 2013, 90% back to my baseline. Time had facilitated the healing process. Two days after, Nyanjera and I quickly caught up on the bus headed towards school. For some reason, Nyanjera seemed to look 'different'. Without being able to pinpoint the exact emotional descriptor, I asked how she was doing. She reported she was fine and then asked me about my holidays. I quickly recounted my holiday activities and concluded that I had more or less arrived at some resolution surrounding my father's death. I asked her about her holidays which she dismissed as being unimpressive. Sensing something was completely off, this time I pushed for more details after which she acknowledged that her aunt had passed away during the holiday but she was not particularly close to that Aunt. She also revealed that a lot of 'family stuff' was going on but will not elaborate further. Knowing Nyanjera valued her privacy, I stopped pushing for more details.

For the rest of our trip, we talked about the resumption of school work and our exercises which she absolutely looked forward to. But then, something drastically changed during our workouts. The constants of these very much anticipated exercises were the personal trainer and the intensity of the exercises. There was a reversal of the enthusiasm towards work out sessions. Nyanjera showed up for exercises mostly late, and less frequently. When she did, she was more quiet and reserved. She still looked very 'different' as though she was upset. The roles were reversed, this time around, I was the one who coaxed her on and encouraged her to stay through the whole session.

One day I abruptly halted our work out session and asked her in an alarming voice, 'Nyanjera what is going on? You are not yourself'. Reaching the bring of frustration, I continued to pepper her with questions for which she would give very brief and non specific answers to. She assured me it was just the pressure of school. Our first board exams where coming up after all, which happened to be a career defining exam. The higher you scored the more competitive you were and had more specialization options for residency (physician training after medical school graduation). The stress of school work and exam prep was taking a toll on all of us. So I agreed and validated her feelings, assuring her she was not alone and trying to console her.

Closer to the end of semester, as exams were quickly drawing near, Nyanjera and myself jointly agreed we were too stressed out to continue our work out. So we stopped going to the gym altogether. The temperatures stayed in the mid 90's our last few weeks of school. Given there were hardly any more small group study meetings to attend, it was not uncommon to skip class because you were assured a class recording to catch up with lectures. This allowed you to create and follow your individual timetable for preparation of the board exams which had to be completed within 2 months of completing this semester. It was not uncommon to go one or two weeks without seeing or talking with your peers.

Everyone was in 'survival mode' burning the midnight oil to optimize their performance for both end of semester exams and board exams. I seldom saw Nyanjera. The one time I ran into her after almost 2 weeks, we were walking in opposite directions. I was headed to class while she was headed to the beach to take a 'breather' promising to catch up with online lessons later on. A few days later, I saw her at a distance heading away from me but too far to catch up with. Maybe she was headed for the beach once more. That day, she looked like she had aged an additional 2-3 years. She was wearing her hair in an orange Mohawk which I thought was quite odd. I wondered how she was doing but I was running late for class. So instead of chasing her, I made a mental note to tell her exactly what I thought about her new hair color, it looked crazy, what was she thinking? And I headed to class.

During our last conversation, Nyanjera told me she was looking forward to the end of the semester which had been so rough besides 'dealing with a lot of family things'. By this time, I had come to understand reference to family struggles was a hint on not to push for more details. She also mentioned she had ended things with Sam but would not elaborate further. She was looking forward to her sister coming to Grenada one week before our exams. They intended to do some light traveling following the end of the semester, prior to preparing and taking the dreaded Board exams in 2 months. It therefore came as a surprise when I later learned that her sister, Akinyi had arrived at the airport and Nyanjera was not there to pick her up.

After several unsuccessful phone call attempts, Akinji hailed a cab to the school campus which she had never been to, but figured she could find anyone on campus who knew Nyanjera. Ironically, the first two people she came across upon walking into a campus study hall were Nyanjera's ex-boyfriend Sam, and his best friend Elvis. They also attempted calling Nyanjera several times but to no avail. They agreed it was strange she was not picking up her phone. Given Akinyi did not know her way around, Sam and Elvis kindly opted to take her to Nyanjera's apartment. So all three headed towards Nyanjera's apartment in Elvis' car.

Upon arrival, they knocked first lightly, and then louder and incessantly pounding on the door when there was no response. At this point everyone suspected something was wrong. But maybe Nyanjera was away from the apartment, sleeping or studying with ear plugs etc. Elvis, announced he knew how to pick locks and with Akinyi's blessing, he successfully unlocked the door. He swung the door open and what he saw made him abruptly stop in his tracks, making Akinyi and Sam who were closely following behind run into him. Elvis immediately pushed everyone backwards to protect them from the site ahead, but it was too late. Everyone had seen Nyanjera's lifeless body on her knees, with her upper body on the bed. One end of the belt encircled her neck while the other end was attached to the bed frame. No one had heard from or seen Nyanjera for 3 days at this time, so it was initially not clear how long Nyanjera had been gone for.

The next day, all over Grenada, there were whispers among the locals who sought to clarify the events surrounding Nyanjera's death. By now, the story was varied with several different accounts of the event. After investigation, the local police concluded that there was no foul play and Nyanjera had taken her life on her own terms. There was no suicidal note, Nyanjera was just...gone. How did I not see this coming? I asked Stacy as we cried after Jackson had delivered the news the day Nyanjera's body was found. It was now evident the 'difference' in Nyanjera I had been identifying for months but could not put a finger on was depression. Maybe the beach visits and work out sessions were all in attempts to overcome her feelings of depression.

Apart from her close friend who happened to be out of town for her father's death, I was the only other person who could have made a difference. I desperately searched my mind for any suicidal tendencies that I might have missed, but nothing stood out. In so many ways we were going through a similar experience, Nyanjera's being the most severe form, but now with very different outcomes. Even though I had never considered suicide, I could see how someone would want to end that painful deep emotional turmoil at any cost once entrapped in it. Nyanjera was extremely private and was suffering a lot and unfortunately all on her own. As a medical student, I had failed to recognize depression or understand it's deadly long term consequences. I had abandoned Nyanjera in her time of need and despite hints given. Consequently, it felt like I had watched her take her own life before me. If I had done or said something, just maybe she would still be around. The old wounds healed a few months ripped open at this realization. The guilt was gnawing at me and unbearable. I was disappointed in myself, in my ability to be a healer and in my ability to be a good friend.

It was a difficult period for all of us who knew and interacted with Nyanjera. Given how horrible we were feeling, I could only imagine what Nyanjera's family was going through. Most especially Akinyi who had possibly witnessed the most painful site she could never erase from her memory. We had a memorial service on the school campus with her family. Sam thanked all of Nyanjera's friends for coming and commented on everyone she had considered her friend. When it came my turn, Sam remarked that Nyanjera was always grateful to me for always respecting her privacy and for being a great listener. 'And look where it got us', was my mental response to this remark. I choked back tears thinking if I had a hunch that Nyanjera was depressed and suicidal, I sure would have pressed on for more details and dragged her to a counselor screaming and kicking if I had to.

Instead, I rationalized and attributed her feelings to the rigor of medical school which was not un- common for the average medical student. Then there were all sorts of disjointed thoughts rummaging my brain. For instance, I thought for goodness sake, she wanted to be a psychiatrist. She of all people should have been aware of her situation given how passionate she was about treating people suffering from mental illness. She should have immediately sort the right help once she started having suicidal thoughts. At this point I was bitter, angry and blamed everyone for her death. First and foremost I blamed myself for missing it, Nyanjera for suffering alone, and my medical school for not having a depression screening tool for this very vulnerable group of medical professionals. If there was some screening in place, there is a possibility Nyanjera would have obtained the help she needed and the outcome will be consequently different.

Nyanjera's family invited us for a funeral service at a chapel in Grenada. Nyanjera laid in a white casket with a wig placed on her head which was different from her usual look. This was probably an attempt to cover the bright orange mohawk she wore prior to her death. I wondered if that hairdo was a bold and outward cry for help I had dismissed as I rushed off to class. She however looked peaceful. Looking at her, I prayed that she would forgive me for not being there for her and hoped that she had now found peace. Her family delivered emotional speeches about Nyanjera's short life on earth and all of her amazing accomplishments so far. The plan was a cremation after which the family intended to take her remains with them to Kenya. Throughout the service, I cried continuously for my young friend's promising and short life and for my father's life cut short. It was one big swirl of emotions.

Psychiatry was my first rotation in New York during my third year of medical school. This is when I fully comprehended everything concerning depression. My second assigned patient had been admitted to my ward for an attempted suicide which had fortunately been unsuccessful. Now very versed with depression and almost as a compensatory mechanism, I passionately took care of my patient. At the end of my rotation, my patient gave me a hug telling me she was grateful for how I listened, counseled her and was always there for her every step of the way. I hugged her back tightly telling her it was my pleasure and to take care of herself. Thinking of Nyanjera, I quickly said my goodbyes and walked away briskly hoping she had not seen the tears that were welling up in my eyes.

Years after Nyanjera's passing, now equipped with knowledge and advice from friends and family, I learned to forgive myself. Introspectively, depression can be likened to a malignant tumor which ravages the organ of origin, spreading through the body like wildfire and eventually deadly if not addressed in a timely manner. After experiencing several close relatives and friends suffer from depression, I was able to draw three lessons from my personal experience:

1) You have to acknowledge there is a problem.
2) You have to be willing to do something about it.
3) Where there is a will, there is a way, consequently you have to act (by seeking help and executing changes) in order to prevent possible dire outcomes.

If your loved one is an adult, you cannot force them through any of the above three steps. Avoid being their therapist in addition to being their designated friend or family member. It is not your job and should be deferred to the experts. As helpless as this sounds, you can be a support to them, encouraging change and providing useful resources that can enact that change. Remind your loved one of the beauty in life and why it is worth fighting for. If your loved one is suicidal, they urgently need hospitalization at the hospital to prevent death. Depression should not be stigmatized. Knowledge is power. We should feel emboldened to address it head on when it rears its ugly head.

Acknowledgment

To all the strong women in my family specifically Esther (mom) , Mary (aunt), you have instilled in me persistence, resilience and problem solving skills which have brought me a long way. Thank you.

Dr. Clarisse Tallah

Clarisse Tallah MD, was born and raised in Yaounde, capital of Cameroon, Africa and immigrated to the United States in 2006. She later on completed an undergraduate Biomedical Engineering degree from Georgia Institute of Technology, Atlanta, Georgia. Dr. Tallah graduated cum laude from Saint George's University School of Medicine, St. George's Grenada through the Keith B. Taylor Global Scholars Program based in Northumbria University, New Castle Upon Tyne, United Kingdom. Dr. Tallah trained at the family medicine residency program in New York University Langone Brooklyn during which she received a recognition for scholarly activity. She is the co-author of 4 research articles and contributed an article in the New York State Family Physician.

She is currently pursuing a maternity care fellowship at the Landmark Medical Center, Woonsocket, Rhode Island while also pursuing a Master's degree in public health from Brown University, Providence, Rhode Island. She hopes to join the fight in decreasing the ever growing maternal mortality related to child birth.

Outside of medicine, Dr. Tallah is a prolific Salsa dancer with occasional indulgence in Tango and Hustle. She also enjoys traveling the world to experience different cultures.

Dr. Anita Sangong
International Medical Graduate

SINGLE MOTHER TO MEDICINE

"I know God won't give me anything I can't handle. I just wish he didn't trust me so much".

~ Mother Teresa

A rickety old brown mud building stared at me. The thatched roof was lopsided and tilted from the incessant onslaught of years of rainfall. Inside the house were two unequal size rooms. The larger one served as a living room. Right in the center was an area for cooking and keeping warm during the harsh cold harmattan months. There was no television, no bookshelf, no dining table. Only a fireplace consisting of three stones and some sprigs leaping with flames as a black pot cooked up a delicious aroma. The earthen floors were hardened from years of stomping unlike the dusty variation whipping up gusts of dirt in the courtyard. The smaller room was a bedroom with three tiny bamboo beds festooned with straw mattresses certain to suck away the sleep from a bewildered body. I stood there transfixed by the sight of it all. Grandma had said I could have a bed all to myself! I jumped atop one of the beds and looked around filled with excitement like the buzzing of a beehive set on fire. This was my fourth move in my lifetime. I was six years old.

The beginning…

My mother was a teenage mother; so young, so naïve and so in love with a young man who would leave her pregnant to chase his dream in faraway America. But she was tenacious and did not allow that to stop her from pursuing her dreams. At barley 9 months old, mama left me with my aunt to return to school. She would only come back for me six years later to take me to a new place I will call home.

My new hometown boasted a little taste of modernization. It was even wired with telephone lines which meant I got to talk to my father more often. Unfortunately, mama and I didn't have a telephone in our home but our neighbor did. I lived for those moments when I would make my way over to our neighbor's house for father's call. I would fidget with excitement as we awaited his call and jump to answer the phone at the very first; so eager was I to hear my daddy's voice.

My father was my hero. His voice sent down effervescent ripples of euphoria down my spine. His vivacious personality was a big part of why I loved him so. He told the best stories that would leave me all giddy in excitement, and all breathless with giggles and laughter. He was serious too and did not hesitate to shape my mind even at a young age. "You will become a doctor", he blurted out one day. I was 6 years old, hardly in a place to be making life's major decisions but daddy said it, so it must be true. From that moment on, a light bulb sparked in my head and I knew and purposed it in my heart to become a doctor when I grew up.

My Grandma, my role-model

After a little while with mama and I was forced to move again, this time to be with my grandmother. I was super excited. I loved my grandma and as expected my years with grandma were pure bliss. Three years of untainted undiluted love. Grandma was strong, hard-working, and the most independent woman I had ever met. She was my role model, my best friend. Memories of my life with my grandma are often very rife. The scent of dust mixed with rainwater after a sudden burst of downpour on a sweltering hot afternoon; my weary legs as I returned from an arduous journey to the river, deep within the forest amidst a barrage of mosquitoes, to fetch clean spring water; my friends laughing, singing, sometimes fighting, as we played under the luminescence of a full moon from a starry sky; my delight in her nightly folklore until an ebony abyss claimed my eyes and I was off to dreamland. Ah, these were good times!

Remarkably, it was with grandma that I started my educational journey towards becoming a medical doctor. Five days a week I trekked on rocky isolated roads to and from school since we couldn't afford the luxury of cars. Many a-nights, my homework was done under the crude fragrance of kerosene from a weak flame flickering through the blurred glass of our old and wobbly lantern. As I endured my daily routine of waking up at the crack of dawn to complete my chores and make it to school on time without receiving the fusillade of lashings for late coming, I learned-learned hard work, endurance, patience, and punctuality; all qualities of a great doctor, though unbeknown to me.

Some days, while my friends hop-scotched and jump rope after school, I had to cross big rivers with overflowing currents deep into a dense forest to assist my grandma on the farm. Without the food from the farm, we will otherwise go hungry. These were my worst days with grandma. The stillness of the forest with the occasional animal's shrill was nothing but scary and my imagination ran wild. Was that the sound of someone running towards me? Or was that the sound of my own labored breathing? With trembling legs, I would sprint on, shivering with shallow breaths as I struggled in muffled inhalation to make it to grandma's comforting weathered face.

Worse was crossing the rivers and streams. Sometimes the river was only knee-deep, and you could stroll across it.

Other times, it was at full flood, swollen with rain and running fast with flowing currents. The powerful current could easily knock anyone off their feet and carry them away. Attempting to swim was ludicrous. Besides, where would you keep all your load? grandma and I usually carried the day's harvest and our farming tools. The safest choice therefore were some old dangling bridges which creaked and swayed with every step. Grandma, dexterous as ever, would carry my fear-stricken body on her back, the day's harvest on her head, her tools on one hand and my own harvest on the other like she had an extra pair of hands.

Seeing her selfless acts of love, how else could I learn to be anything but empathetic? I was fortunate to have socks and shoes to wear to school while the other village children walked barefoot to school every day. Feeling like the odd one out, I decided to also start going barefoot to school in a show of solidarity much to the dismay of grandma. To make her happy, I wore my shoes and socks when I left home for school but with childlike mischief quickly removed and hid them by the side of the road as soon as I was out of sight only to wear them again on my way back. By some stroke of luck, grandma was none the wiser of my little antics.

By the time I was nine years old, my life was disrupted yet again as I trudged from grandmother's house to the city to live with my aunt. I spent the next three years of my life there, completing and finishing primary school before being shipped off to boarding school for middle and high school.

A new kind of life

St. Bede's College, Ashing - Cameroon was elitist with near perfect passing rates in all public standardized exams. I had never met my father in person, but he was as invested in my education as any father could be. Boarding school came at a whopping 200,000FCFA (about $400) tuition cost which per Cameroonian standards was a small fortune. My father was a fulltime student in America, working only part-time and earning a measly $3.50/hour. Yet, he scrapped ends and sent my tuition every year; even if I had to be sent home many times during the school year for delayed payment.

Meanwhile, life on campus was a whole 'nother' ball game. Boarding school was a society all on its own with a stratified class system. I was one of the poor students, holding claim to very limited cash allowance and homemade goodies to sustain me every term. 2000FCFA (about $4) was all I had to my name every term but I made it stretch far. Grandma raised no prodigal. Besides, I always considered myself extremely blessed and remained ever grateful for the opportunity to be enrolled in such a prestigious institution.

Welcome to the USA

After three years in St. Bede's College, my mother and I won the Diversity Lottery visa to travel to the USA. Me, America? My parents together again? This was my biggest childhood dream - to live with both my parents under the same roof. I had prayed for this for as long as I could remember, and here I was, about to live it. Talk about faith in action. No wonder the Holy Book speaks of faith as "the substance of things hoped for, the evidence of things not seen." (Hebrews 11:1 NKJV).

I was counting down the days to when we would travel to the US and I finally get to see my father face-to-face. The day came and I was a basket case of excitement. First time on an airplane and I reveled in the novelty of it all. 18-hour flight but I couldn't sleep a wink. I was just that excited to meet my daddy although I wasn't sure what to expect. Well guess what? Daddy showed up, not only by himself but with a whole entourage of his friends with balloons, flowers, cameras, limousine ride, and later, a big party at home…I mean, all the bells and whistles of the welcome party of highly esteemed guests. In that moment, I fell in love even more with this man who already held such a big part of my heart.

Everything was so perfect for the first three weeks of my new life in the US. Our apartment was plush! A far cry from the homes I lived in in Cameroon. I had my own room and bathroom for the first time in my life, and our perfect little family thrived on its newfound togetherness. Exotic lunches and dinners where my mother and I tasted delicacies we couldn't even pronounce, shopping trips where I learned the difference between a dime and a nickel, long road trips across multiple state lines - you name it, we did it. It was a thing of fairytales and I could only hope for a happy ever after ending.

Life with my Father

Life, it would seem, is not the stuff fairy tales are made of. Or perhaps, familiarity breeds contempt. I would never know. All I know is that after the idyllic three weeks with my father, things started to degenerate with water trickling speed as I saw the side of my father I was unprepared for. I was a teenager as temperamental as they come; and he was a parent, as strict as they come. My daddy was your typical alpha male; fastidious, unbending and headstrong, it was his way or the highway. Clean the house - but there's a speck of dust left untouched there. Do the dishes - the stainless steel wasn't polished to sparkling shine. Laundry done - the clothes were not ironed to crisp perfection. It was never a thank you or a job well done.

Please don't get me started on our regular "meetings"! I thought of them as mini-court sessions: 2 hours long where I was apprised of all my wrongdoings. At least, with a court trial the defendant has time to defend themselves; not so in my case. My judge never granted me audience to speak. Worse still, it was rude and disrespectful to talk back to my parent, I was told. So, in humble dejection I listened on as I was washed down, my silent sobs my only response and my promise to do better the only words I would utter. Even when I slumbered, there was no rest as I would be woken up many times to answer to for all my wrongdoings. So accustomed to his berating that wherever he called my name, the first thing out of my mouth was, "did I do something wrong?" I was living in a constant state of anxiety and would suffer from bouts of unexplainable heart palpitations that landed me in the hospital at least three times.

Twice a failure

Daddy was an academic so good grades were his expectation of me. I delivered but that was about where it ended. When it came to my career, we butted heads over my career path. He wanted a two-year college, I dreamed of a full-blown collegiate experience in a 4-year university. He won. He wanted a career in nursing, I said medicine. He won again, somewhat. I was left bewildered and dejected. Wasn't this the same man who had predicted that I would be a doctor?

Begrudgingly, I enrolled in a community college like my father wanted. But I was a wise little thing alright; I made sure I only took those courses that satisfied the requirements for entry into both nursing and medical school programs. No one would kill my dreams, even if that person was my father.

After completing the first year in community college, I applied and was accepted into the community college nursing program with an excellent GPA. I was even granted a scholarship which paid for my entire tuition for one semester. However, considering my challenges living at home with my dad, compounded with the fact that my father did not allow me to get a driver's license nor drive while I was enrolled in nursing school, nursing school was extremely stressful. Consequently, I failed just shy of 0.03% and was kicked out of the program! Oh well, maybe nursing wasn't for me after all. I spent the remaining year completing courses and graduated with an Associate's Degree in General Studies.

Graduating with an associate's degree was a huge boost to my ego. I was once again convinced of my ability to succeed. Again, with pressure from my dad, I gave nursing another shot. As the Gods will have it, a North Carolina university granted me admission into their nursing program. I figured, Ok, he gets his nursing, and I will get my university experience – we will call it a truce, everyone's happy. Well surprise, surprise…Daddy said no again; if I dared to make that journey out of state come fall, he would disown me. I loved my father too much to risk such a separation from him. So, again I acquiesced; He won.

I enrolled in a community college nursing program again, and passed the nursing entrance exam with flying colors. I gave up my dreams of dorm life and embraced my reality of off-campus living. I had a driver's license now but still no car. Daddy came up for me too and rented a room for me in a townhouse shared by two other students. However, I had no internet, no computer, or even a study table. The house was nowhere near any bus stop, so I had to rely on rides from roommates and schoolmates to make it to classes and clinicals. During times when they were not so benevolent, I had to break the bank for cab fares. I eventually saved up enough and with the support from my parents bought a 1973 Honda Accord. It was a wobbly, unreliable old thing that became my mode of transportation to school; on the days when it started, that is.

My second attempt at nursing school would come when I was still battling a distressed home life. The relationship with my father was deteriorating with every passing day and the pain of that consumed me more than my nursing books did. With the in-fighting at home at an all-time high with my dad, I failed again by the end of that first semester in the nursing program. I was kicked out, yet again.

I tell you, nursing school is stressful even in the most comfortable of circumstances. Try doing that when battling a turbulent home life; when you have no driver's license and public transportation is all you rely on to get to early morning classes; with the fear of failure and the inability to satisfy a hard-to-please parent hanging over your head and nursing school becomes almost impossible to bear. At least that was my story.

Not being one to give up easily, I applied to yet another nursing school and was accepted. My father tried to get involved but I shunned all help from him but for the $1000 he gifted me at the beginning of my first semester. Don't ask me how I planned on raising the $18,000 tuition looming ahead of me. I had no idea but I knew for certain I wanted no help from my father. Also, this time around, I was determined to finish the program. I had a driver's license and a fully functioning car which was a plus. My mind was made up that I would complete the program to make my father happy. Then, I will head on straight to medical school in fulfillment of my own lifelong dream of becoming a medical doctor.

By this time, I was working as a Patient Care Technician (PCT) at a local hospital. I loved the job and realized I had a knack and passion for helping people. Most importantly, my job loved me too, so much so I was offered a full scholarship which paid for my tuition throughout the nursing program in exchange of a 20-hour minimum a week commitment. It was a very easy bargain to make. I tackled nursing school with a ferocious level of seriousness which was unusual even for one as studious as myself.

Disowned...

Halfway into my program, my parents separated. I ended up living with my dad fulltime while attending classes. It wasn't too long before my dad could not pay the rent all by himself and took in a roommate to cut cost. This meant me giving up my room. My dad asked me to move out a few weeks just before my course exam. Dad's decision couldn't have come at a worse time, but I honestly understood where he was coming from, and empathized with his plight. I moved out and decided not to let the move be a distraction.

By my last semester, I was so engrossed with my studies with an even deeper determination to succeed that I stopped answering my calls. Yes, all calls, not even from daddy dearest. He was none too pleased, as you can very well imagine. When I eventually graduated and passed my board exam as a Registered Nurse (RN), I hoped that all would soon be forgotten. The end had justified the means. No siree! My father was livid and disowned me. All my pleas for forgiveness fell on deaf ears. Every attempt at peacemaking, even as recent as May 2018, has been futile till this day.

Engaged: I'm going to be married!

One year after graduating as an RN, as if everything was lining up in my favor, I met the love of my life. Like it happened only yesterday, I remember the first day we met. He showed up at my apartment for us to go on our first date. I did a double, even triple take when I opened the door to find this specimen of male beauty standing outside my door. Ahhhhh, those eyes!!! They were orb round and soft, mesmerizing and sparkling with warmth and the vigor of youth at every flutter. His deep intense stares under scythe-shaped eyebrows held me captive and his voice left me weak at the knees. He was the strong silent type that unintentionally drew women to him and I fell head over heels in love with a schoolgirl's crush. Oh and his walk! His walk was a saunter as he glided with an athletic grace that will make any woman swoon. His only blemish was that he was of average countenance, not tall but not short either.

However, for what he lacked in height, he made up in charm especially with the swirl of his loamy cologne that constantly had me in a daze of desire. Ours was a match made in *Cameroonian heaven*. He was my warmth, security, love, encouragement, motivation, happiness, my hope. He completely filled the emptiness and void that I always had since when I was a child. My heart skipped whenever I heard his husky voice that seemed to deepen a notch just for me. What more? He was interested in a career in medicine like I was. In fact, ours was a match made in *Cameroonian medicine heaven*.

After two years of dating, I became pregnant. Four months later, he proposed. Wait, was this really happening to me? First love, then a baby and now marriage! If this was a dream, I never wanted to wake up. I also wasn't going to question what I ever did to deserve all these blessings. I was happy and grateful for them all the same. At 38 weeks I became the proud mother of the most beautiful baby girl. And just like that, I fell in love all over again; this time to a tiny human being with the not-so-tiny lungs!

Single Motherhood

Good times they say, do not last forever. My joy turned out to be very short lived. By the time our baby was seven months old, the engagement failed, and I had to move out of yet another home in search for new living quarters. This time around though, I had a fussy infant in tow. Twice I had been forced out of a house I called my home. Twice, by the men I love. The first time, by my father. The second time, by my fiancé! Was I cursed or what?

As one who had been cheated out of fatherly presence for the greater part of my life, I knew firsthand the pain of growing up without a father. I knew how it felt to be unable to throw out the "I will tell my daddy" threat to a surly bully. I knew how it felt growing up with constant feelings of abandonment due to the profound absence of a parent. I knew all this and did not want that for my daughter. Thus, I swallowed my pride and I initiated a reconciliatory meeting; just like I had done with my father. I even apologized for things I didn't even know I did. Still he was not willing to budge so for me and my daughter's sake, I picked up the pieces of my broken life and bowed out comforted by the words of scripture: "My grace is sufficient for you, for My strength is made perfect in weakness" (2 Cor. 12:9 NKJV).

Starting all over

We started our life all over again - my girl and I. There was a roof over our head, warm clothes on our back and enough food in our belly and for this I was mightily grateful as we lived one day at a time. Some days were hard, childcare was expensive and medical school was even harder. My mother tried to help whenever she could, I had to make very huge sacrifices but ultimately we survived and we thrived.

Being a parent, and a single one at that was motivation enough for me to be all I had ever desired to be. Who wouldn't want to hear that tootsie innocent voice squeal in excitement "mama you did it!" It almost feels like she was sent forth to give me a new lease and renewed confidence in life: to see her first step, watch her first fall, cheer at her first dance recital, beam at her graduation, and weep for joy at her wedding. Knowing these things don't come cheap and determined to provide my daughter the best in life, this girl started making plans to increase her earnings even while pursuing her passion - hello medicine.

Doctor at last!

I chose Washington University of Health and Science, Belize. Going to medical school was an extremely trying time as I depleted all my savings of several years to pay out of pocket. It was heart wrenching to hear the sobs of my baby begging me not to leave and it was especially lonely for me to spend so many months away from this mini-me who had become my only daily companion. As for child care? Had medical school tuition not crippled me, childcare would have. Ridiculously expensive is the only way I can describe this bill, which cost much more than I was required to dole out every month for room and board. Ultimately, it paid off and many years after my father first told me I would become a doctor, I eventually did. I am one very proud MD and excited about my journey to residency.

Lessons Learned

Becoming a doctor is a journey of a few years for some which ended up being a journey of many years for me. But who cares? It is a journey completed all the same and along the way, I learned lifelong lessons.

Fortitude

Defined as the strength of mind and soul to withstand adversity and suffering. Need I say my life was faced with obstacles and astronomical odds stacked up against me? Interestingly, when your pain or hardship is great or long-lasting you are more susceptible to collapsing under its weight. However, never allow your pain consume you. More so, you should never ever give up on your dreams. Your dreams should be your reason to keep on striving. The greatest physicians who truly understand and give the best holistic care to their patients are the ones who have had so many failures in life. Out of these failures you learn endurance, patience, tolerance which compound together as fortitude.

Gratitude

I owe this lesson to my grandma. Grandma was always very appreciative of everything even the littlest things. Above all, she was always grateful for life itself. Basic human needs such as clothes, shoes, food, clean drinking water, plumbing and electricity, cars, and even the perfectly tarred roads, meant little or nothing to Grandma. In the hardship of her village life, she was content and grateful. Having a spirit of gratitude always, helps to harness a positive energy and vibe which translates into all aspects of your life. Always be grateful!

Teamwork

Another valuable lesson from Grandma. Navigating the scary rivers in the village with Grandma was one of my first lessons on teamwork. We will share our load to make sure our balance was even when we started across the frail dangly bridge. The goal was, when Grandma carried my frightened self on her back, we could all focus on one task: crossing the river safely and nothing else. Teamwork, I realized is a valuable life skill and an absolute-must skill in the profession of Medicine. Thank you Grandma.

Communication

My relationship with my father and my fiancé, taught me the importance of communication. Be it between spouses, parents and children, family members, friends, and coworkers, communication is invaluable. Having open-ended conversations, being open to suggestions, and allowing everyone to express their opinions, thoughts, feelings and recommendations is very therapeutic. This leads to stronger and more meaningful relationships where everyone co-exists peacefully despite apparent and muted differences.

Forgiveness

The ultimate lesson I learned through my experiences is forgiveness. It takes strength to forgive and forgiving gives you enormous strength in return. I have learned how to forgive myself. I have learned that no one is perfect and we all make mistakes. Most importantly, I have learned to have peace within me at all times. This has helped me to cope with the harrowing experiences that I have faced in my life. Usually, after a breakup, we sometimes want to retaliate either by hating our ex or badmouthing them. In fact, we sometimes, go as far as wanting to show our greatness to our ex and making them lament over leaving us. The question you should ask yourself during such a time is, "Why?" Why is this necessary? What difference will it make? Forgive them and move on. It is not only a sign of maturity but a sign of strength.

Moving Forward…

While my life has not been a bed of sweet-smelling roses, I have continued on forward instead of trying to repair the past, which is impossible to change. In life, some things are just inevitable while others can be changed through hard work and courage. Identify the things you can control and those you can't control. Change the things you can control and leave those you can't control in the hands of your God. Don't whine about hardships. They will only diminish your spirit. Embrace hardships and use them to forge ahead. From childhood to single parenthood, my hardships have been infinite, however, they have matured me and reaffirmed my positive outlook of circumstances and of people.

Life is beautiful and is for the living. Live it to the fullest. Let nothing hold you down!

ACKNOWLEDGMENT

I dedicate this chapter to God almighty and some selfless pastors He strategically placed in my path to help me sail through my challenges.

Dr. Anita Sangong

Dr. Anita Sangong is a healthcare professional with over 11 years of clinical experience. Born in Cameroon where she spent her childhood, Dr. Sangong immigrated to the United States in 1999. Pursuing a lifelong ambition for a career in medicine, she obtained an Associate's degree in General Studies (2005) from Montgomery College, Takoma Park; and an Associate of Science in Nursing degree (2008) from Radians College, Washington DC. In 2016, she graduated with honors from Washington University of Health and Science, Belize with a Doctor of Medicine (MD) degree.

While awaiting residency placement in Internal Medicine or Dermatology, Dr. Sangong continues to serve her patients as a Registered nurse. She is an ardent philanthropist and is dedicated to giving back to her community. Ever cognizant of her roots too, Dr. Sangong hopes to someday provide free healthcare services to impoverished communities in Cameroon's hinterlands where she grew up.

When she is not wearing the hat of the dedicated nurse and physician, Dr. Sangong is simply "mom" to beautiful 7-year-old Lisa who is tied to her hip. Anita and Lisa love to spend time together reading, dancing, trying out new recipes, singing, participating in church activities, watching too many cartoons, throwing balls at the beach and everything silly.

Dr. Sangong is also co-author of the page-turner, *Beyond Challenges*, which chronicles the stories of 15 female immigrant physicians who beat the odds and soared through hardships that threatened their careers in medicine.

Dr. Irene Bih Wakam
Board Certified Family Medicine

Always be Optimistic

We are products of our upbringing. It is imperative to take an inventory of one's childhood to understand how we approach life and be comfortable. We don't live in a vacuum. Our decisions are based on past experiences whether or not consciously. I am a minority on several fronts but that does not define me. I am a black woman with a different accent originally from Cameroon in West Africa. Women raised me. My mother was a teenager when she conceived me out of wedlock with a married man, who had several wives and children. Her family refused to let him marry her. I was raised by my mother, Aunt(her older sister) and maternal grandmother. My father owned a construction company and was very successful. He lived in a large estate with his wives and children. He was well known in our town because his company built many prominent buildings.

My early education was mostly in female Catholic schools. The first seven years were in elementary school and the last five years in a Girls' boarding school, Our Lady of Lourdes Secondary School, ran by Irish Reverent sisters. I had two years of co-ed education in a boarding high school and from there migrated to the United States to continue my education. My early years define the woman I am today. I had no anonymity growing up because in my home town my father was well known. He was considered "rich" but I was growing up with my poor mothers and was being judged by others. My stepmothers complained whenever they saw me, saying I was a disgrace to my father because I was not 'flashy' like my half-sisters who were always roaming around town in Range Rovers or Mercedes cars during the holidays.

My father tried his best to reassure me that he was proud of me because I was smart and that we were all his children and he treated us the same. He and his wives and children lived in a large Estate that I hated to visit because of the scrutiny and being asked stupid questions when he was not around. All these made me determined to succeed and prove that I was better.

At the age of 14 my father asked me not to visit the house when he was not present because of a confrontation I had with my stepmother. I stopped going there and only returned several years later as an adult, after his death. In retrospect, I consider myself lucky for making that decision because it was a toxic environment for a young child with no protection. There was a lot of turmoil going on in that household and unfortunately, I was an easy target.

I learned very early in life to defend myself. I was teased mercilessly in boarding school and to defend myself I became very outspoken and aggressive. Instinctively, I developed a response for any insult or tease, never letting myself become vulnerable. That has carried on into my personal life which can be difficult for those close to me.

I have had to defend myself even for things which I have no control over such as my birth. The choice was either to let people treat me as inferior or a mistake or stand up for myself. I choose the latter. This has made it easy for me to cope in the United States with all the discrimination. I prefer to be a leader not follow anyone blindly. It was not always easy in a Catholic Boarding School. The Reverent sisters considered me rebellious because I questioned Catholicism. For example, I stopped going to confession because I did not get a logical answer as to why one has to go through a priest to confess to God. In retrospect I was classified as being stubborn when I was just being an inquisitive teenager. It will surprise those Reverent sisters to know that I am still spiritual and I listened to a lot of the lessons about life they tried to instill on us. I consider my time in Our Lady of Lourdes College, the best formative years and I am grateful to them.

My life in the United States has not been as challenging because it has been a continuum from the life lived in Cameroon. I believe in working hard and following my dreams. I came here from high school to do medicine. My father told me to do medicine and I never question it. My mentor and role model in the family was in the medical field when I left Cameroon. Hence it was natural for me to follow in her footsteps. I did not understand the American system on arrival. I had to do an undergraduate degree before applying for admission to medical school.

Every Cameroonian I met discouraged me from doing medicine. I was told it was very difficult for foreigners to get admission into medical school. I took that as a challenged to do it. I was confident I could do it especially after a few workers in a Nursing home where I worked mocked me when I said I wanted to be a physician. They laughed and said they also wanted to be the president. I am sure they are still doing the same job there. Undergraduate education was easy for me because the tests were all multiple choice. My greatest obstacle was the laboratory tests. My first hour in a chemistry lab in the United States is still unforgettable. I could not believe there was fire without using a match and no Bunsen burner. Gas coming out from the wall with no gas tank.

Unfortunately for me, there were few African American students in the classes so I did not know how to approach my white classmates. In biology, I did not have a partner in the lab until an African American student walked in late. We have been friends for over 30 years going. She is a Gynecologist and I consider her a sister.

I am glad I pursued medicine because it was easy to get in. I applied to three schools and got admitted into all of them. I hand wrote my application because I did not know how to type. I later found out the main reason foreigners at the time had difficulties was their GPA and MCAT scores because most of them were working and going to school so it was difficult but they were not being honest. Granted finances could have been a deterrent after gaining admission. Medical school was very difficult for me. It was the first time in life that I studied and did not do well. Before then I believe to succeed all one needed to do was study. I spend hours studying and my best was average. I failed the comprehensive examination at the end of my first year and that floored me.

I found out after talking to a consultant which the school provided, that the problem was, I did not know how to speed read because I was never taught. The material was not difficult but the volume of material to cover was intractable. Thus the optimal approach to studying was to focus on what was important. I went into medical school with the prior notion from my Catholic school, which was I had to prioritize attending classes over-allocating sufficient time to study. Even when I had all the notes, I still attended all the classes and did not have enough time left to study. Through talking to the consultant, I also found out about using past tests as a guide to know what to concentrate on. I truly was lost because I did not have friends to get past tests from.

I joined the Black Medical Association but unfortunately, it was not useful to me. People in the group were competing among themselves and were not very generous in sharing ideas. I dropped out of the organization and made friends with an honors student in my lab group Scott, who saved my career. He directed me on how to study and some test-taking skills. Before I became friends with

Scott I was depressed because I did not know how to tell my family that I was not smart enough to become a physician. I felt increasing pressure because my parents and boyfriend told everyone that I was studying to become a physician. Before taking my comprehensive medical school exam, I firmly believed that if one studied there was no room for failure. I honestly would have dropped out of medical school if not of Scott.

In my mind, I was working very hard but no matter what I did I was an average student so I decided to move on with life. I got married and started a family. I got pregnant in my second year and had my daughter at the beginning of the third year.

I had a difficult pregnancy according to my Obstetrician but was too busy to worry. I gain fifty-four pounds but did not notice. I was preeclamptic but did not appreciate the implication. Ignorance is bliss. I had an old, very caring Obstetrician who was very nice to me. I told him I was busy in school and did not have time for prenatal visits. He made my appointments around my classes. He even stayed late some days and let me in through the back door. When I found out later all the complications I could have had, I was happy I did not know. I fought him when he wanted to admit me for induction.

Having a child during my third year in medical school meant I was not available for her. I tried breastfeeding but did not have milk and the pumps those days were a nightmare so I stopped attempting to breastfeed after 3 months. Luckily, as a medical student, we got the baby formula for free from the companies for a year. I had enough to distribute to other mothers in the community. I was fortunate to have a live-in baby-sitter from Cameroon who was a substitute mother for my child. My husband was a hands-on Dad. He took my daughter to all her appointments. I would prepare her food in the morning but did not get home until late. There was one positive thing in having my baby when I did because my first rotation after I got back was Ob/Gyn. I got back in less than 1month so all the patients during labor were excited to have me and followed my instructions. Some of them told the Attending Physician that they preferred me to deliver their baby which was hilarious since I was a mere student. It was great to be needed though I was taking Darvocet for pain every 6 hours because I had bad hemorrhoids.

I was pregnant with my second child during my fourth year of medical school and had him in October of my internship. I could not fit behind the class desk to take the board exam so I had to sit in front of the class. My medical school 'Wayne State University' still has the largest medical class in the country, so we don't know our classmates. Interestingly whenever I meet my classmate and they don't remember me, I remind them I was the student who sad in front of the class during the board exam. The next thing they say is' African woman'. I was the only African in my class and made it a point for them to remember me because I wore African outfits whenever there was a party and a lot of them were invited to my house parties and were excited to eat African food.

My classmates always ask me how many children I have because to them I was pregnant throughout medical school and residency so they expect me to have a large family. I found out physicians, at least those days in the late eighties did not appreciate their colleagues being pregnant. My medical director never said a kind word to me about my pregnancy. He did not congratulate me when I had the baby. I had a full load of patients just like any other Resident which was not a problem. My patients were very kind. There was one incident I remember during a call in the emergency room. I was doing an admission and I must have fallen asleep because I remember the patient asking me whether I wanted coffee. Our calls those days were brutal because now there are some regulations about extended hours.

When I got pregnant again with my last child during my third year of Residency my medical director was outright unfriendly. I worked until I went into labor. I maintained my regular load of patients until the day I went into labor. I was having severe back pain which I did not attribute to labor because I was only 39 weeks and my previous two pregnancies went past 40 weeks. When I called my Director from the hospital the next day after I had my baby, all he asked me was who was covering for me, no congratulations. I could have taken six weeks off to spend time with my baby and make up the two weeks after graduation but he refused to give me permission and those 2 weeks of work were needed to qualify to take my board exam. I knew if I did not go back and waited 6-12 months to take the National Board exam, he would have used my case as a warning to tell the residents not to get pregnant during Residency. I was determined to graduate and take the exam with my colleagues.

He insinuated that being pregnant during residency was not good because there were certain requirements to take the board examination. I did what I had to do to graduate on time and passed the board exam. He told me years later when I visited the program they were not sure I would pass the exam because I was behind compared to my colleagues. He will not dare say that now to a female resident just because they are pregnant. To be fair to him I sometimes look back and wonder how I managed to have children during medical training.

At the time I told them I was an African woman and multitalented, oh, the beauty of youth! I made a change in my career. When I began medical school, my goal was to be a general surgeon or a Gynecologist. Along the way, I got married and have children. My children were all planned. I did family medicine because at the time it was difficult to join a group and work part-time. The surgical residency was also brutal. All the female surgical residents in my hospital switched resident program after the first year. Today patients want female physicians which is so refreshing. In the early '90s, female Obstetricians were having problems getting a partnership in medical groups which were predominantly male groups. Now it is a plus because patients want us. I did Family medicine because I wanted to continue obstetrics and surgery. I wanted to have that option. I did not pursue it because all my deliveries as a resident were at night and I still had a full schedule the next day. Also, malpractice Insurance doing deliveries was too expensive to justify doing it.

It is thirty years now since I graduated medical school and I am doing more Geriatrics. I have evolved with my patients. When I started I did a lot of pediatrics but my practice now has aged with me. I started working in a group practice because I thought it would give me more flexibility and time to raise a family. I later found out that owning your own practice gives you more flexibility but you have to work harder and have to deal with management which you don't think about as an employee. You also have to be knowledgeable about billing and employee rights and legislation which you never worry about working for someone. I have been in solo practice going on 18 years. I moved from Michigan to California and the practice is different in the different states. I had to start all over in California networking and dealing with the different Insurances. I have seen medicine evolve over the years.

Some things good and some not so good. Insurance has more control over the decisions doctors make. Now we also have electronic medical records. I have had to teach myself typing and the computer is still a working progress. I am always ready for a challenge. Patients are becoming more challenging. They have easy access to medical literature which can be good in some aspects, because you can always refer them to websites to look up things. The flip side is they think they have all the answers. They can be less respectful especially depending on where you practice. There are certain preconceived ideas about doctors of foreign descent. It is always interesting when I meet a patient who outright tells me they don't like foreign doctors. They get confused when I ask them to be specific whether they mean foreign like in noncitizen, foreign-trained or what. As long as one is confident in what they are doing or who they are, there is not a problem.

I first encountered the issue in Michigan very early in my career because my partner was a white older physician. Patients always assumed because I had a different accent I was foreign-trained which was a big deal then. My office was a few miles from my medical school and my certificates were hung on the walls. I was constantly asked which medical school I attended. When I tell them they will ask me which one. When I tell them Wayne State in Detroit. A lot of them acted surprised and say' oh that one'. I also had fun asking them where the other one was located. The internet and world news have helped because these days being a foreign doctor is no longer a novelty.

Americans read or hear about discoveries and new treatments for diseases from physicians all over the globe. There are still patients who tell me they want American trained physician and I rarely correct them. I let them go because I know we most likely would not get along.

Medicine is not an exact science . Part of the treatment process is trusting your physician. If a patient has to always second guess the physician, I think that hampers their treatment and they are better off with someone they trust. In my little town, I see patients who come in surprised to see a black physician and are very excited. I have gotten many patients just because they are looking for a female physician. I have only had to dismiss about two patients in my career because they were outright difficult and distrusting. I know my limitations and I am not afraid to pull out my computer to look up something or tell a patient I will get back with them or refer them out. I am honest and direct with every one and this is not always acceptable but I can honestly say people decide quickly when they meet me. It is alright if they don't like me as long as they trust me. I tell a patient who meets me for the first time what my philosophy is in medicine. I work with them but I am not a miracle worker. Their health should be more important to them because it is their life.

There have been a few tragedies in my life that have made a profound impact on my career. The first one was when my father died during my residency, which was very difficult for me to process that he would never see me as a physician. After his death, I was certain I was never going back to Cameroon to practice. The next tragedy was my sister who was only 35 years old when she died in Britain. She was my half-sister who tried to bring some unity in the family. I decided to take her off life support which weighed heavily on my conscience for years because I was not there in person to evaluate her. There was no good explanation for her death. At the time I was working in a group practice and things were not running smoothly. I had just moved to California and was finding out that medical practice was different here. I considered dropping out of medicine because I had done the rounds working for several clinics and was not satisfied. I did not want to die and regret wasting my time in a job I did not enjoy. My kids were young and needed my attention. My husband convinced me to try private practice for five years before giving up. As much as I love medicine, above all, I value my happiness. I am still in solo practice. The last tragedy was the recent death of my younger sister from breast cancer. It is difficult to continue helping others while your family is dying. I have patients with stage IV breast cancer surviving and my sister is gone. Her illness has made me question my purpose in this life.

My children are adults. I am looking at my life and doing a lot of soul searching and I discovered that I no longer want to continue doing medicine in the States. I have always wanted to make a difference and I am not sure I am doing that here. I am trying to transition back to Cameroon. It is difficult because I am caught between two cultures. I relate more to the American way of thinking just because I have been here most of my adult life. I do medical missions in Cameroon annually and I am more involved in the Cameroon community here in California. For the past three years, life has been interesting. I am hearing the same discouragement when I tell Cameroonians I want to move back home like when I told them I wanted to do medicine 30 years ago. Everyone tells me I won't last in Cameroon. There I go again counting on myself. I am not as naive as Cameroonians think. I am experiencing roadblocks even from here.

When I first went there to do volunteer work. I tried registering with the medical council which is the equivalent of the American Medical Association. Gathering the documents took 2 days with someone from the Presidency helping me. After I finally got everything it was rejected because I could not provide my High School certificate. I went to my high school and it is not there and there is no good explanation because there is no evidence that someone picked it up. There is no blueprint on how things are supposed to be done. I get conflicting advice on how to go about doing anything there. I have been trying for the past five years to get a land title on the plot that I plan to do business. To make matters even more complicated, there is a civil war going on. I have never succumbed to any obstacle in my life. I am trying to navigate the two systems. Unfortunately for me, my husband and I were so involved raising the children and did not keep up with activities in the Cameroon community. I now realize that growing up in boarding schools back in Cameroon did not expose me to the culture. It is more difficult to accept some of the things as an adult. Life is interesting!

Three years ago, I volunteered in a hospital in Cameroon for two weeks and I honestly came back wondering whether I can practice there. I have a lot of respect for the attending physician running that hospital. I was impressed to see how much difference he was making in the lives of the people. It was humbling to follow him around for those two weeks. He made me question why I am working here when there is so much need back there. While I was in that hospital, I noticed that there were a lot of activities going on at the mortuary and it got me curious. I went to check how the embalming was done. I could not stay in the prep room for 3minutes because of toxic fumes. I did not know much about it but I knew the environment was hazardous. I decided to do something about it.

When I got back to the States I went to a mortuary school which was more difficult than I thought. I realize it is an area in which I can make a difference, and have the dead be treated respectfully. My idea is to make sure the bodies are embalmed properly without exposing workers to carcinogens, or diseases while dignifying the Mortuary system in Cameroon. I am now a certified Funeral Director and it has been a challenge trying to understand the funeral system in Cameroon. I am looking forward to my new chapter. I have come full circle delivering babies, treating patients and hopefully burying them with dignity. My story is to be continued.

I may be aging in years but not in my dreams. I am optimistic that my best years are ahead. I am still navigating my way through life. I have a lot of projects. I may have to go through detours to get there but, I am more excited about my future now than 30 years ago. Nobody is dependent on me. I don't have to justify my actions. I am wiser and more experienced. I have nothing to prove to anyone. I have a supportive family. I enjoy living and hope to be around to see my grandchildren grow. I believe we are in charge of our destiny. I am not perfect. I believe in learning from my mistakes and moving forward. I am content to be an average mother, grandmother, and physician. I may be a minority but I am not a minor player in life.

ACKNOWLEDGEMENT

Family: I am a proud grandmother, mother of a daughter and two sons and have been married for 35 years. I am very involved in the community and love to travel. I am exploring moving back to Cameroon where I feel I can have the greatest impact on Humanity in Cameroon's hinterlands where I grew up.

Dr. Irene Bih Wakam

I was born on July 12th, 1959 in Mankon, Bamenda Cameroon West Africa to Monica Sirri Neba and Daniel Awah Nangah. I am the first of 3 daughters to my mother.

Education: My elementary education was in *Roman Catholic Mission Girls' school Mankon, Bamenda*. I did my secondary education in *Our Lady of Lourdes Mankon, Bamenda* and finished my high school education at *Cameroon College of Arts and Science Bambili*. I moved to the United States in 1980. I obtained a **B.S.** in Biological Science with distinction from *Wayne State University Detroit Michigan* in the USA. Also obtained a postgraduate degree in medicine from the same institution. I did a three-year residency in **Family Medicine** in *St John's hospital* in Detroit Michigan.

Professional Experience: Upon completion of my residency and passing the Family Practice board certification in 1992, I worked as a primary care provider for 3 years with Metro Medical Group in Roseville, Michigan. I spent another 2 years with Henry Ford Medical Health System in Novi, Michigan. In 1997, I moved with my family to Ventura California. I worked in several private and county clinics providing urgent care, primary care, and industrial medicine services. From 2002 to present I have been running a solo private practice providing primary care to all ages and also doing Immigration physicals as a civil surgeon. For the past five years, I have been involved in several missions to Cameroon and Haiti.

Dr. Grace A. Neba Fobi
Retired Public Health Ophthalmologist

Becoming a better me

Recognizing my purpose:

The amphitheater was packed full of students, professors, parents and friends all gathered for the graduation of the 6th batch of medical doctors from the University Centre for Health Sciences (CUSS)-Yaoundé. I was one of the graduates. This day had finally come! I had not slept for days, not because of the preparations building up to graduation but out of excitement, joy, anticipation and the knowledge that I was soon to be sworn in as a medical Doctor. My dream come true. I suddenly heard my name being called by the Dean: *'Akohobe Neba Grace, Honors table'*. What? Honors table? My heart skipped a beat. I moved up to the stage like in a trance. Family and friends later told me that as I moved up the stage there was some kind of radiance on my face, showing an ear to ear smile. I truly felt happy and proud to have reached this stage in my life. The journey had not been an easy one.

I was born on the third day of our Lord in January 1955 in Bafut, a small village on the hills, in the North West Province of Cameroon. My father was a World War II veteran. From the stories he told us as kids he fought the war in a place called Bombay. Upon returning from the war he was employed as a clerk in the court house and also helped the church as a catechist. My mother was a housewife and had never seen the walls of a classroom though she made sure I did my school homework. She worked hard in her farms producing the foods and vegetables we ate.

My early childhood was full of fun memories. I do not remember going to bed hungry. I was happy and loved going to school with dreams about being a teacher or a tailor when I grew up. I dreamed about living in a big beautiful house surrounded by gardens and flowers. I dreamed of having lots of friends and cars and money etc. My father grew coffee and I vividly remember him roasting coffee beans and making one of the most delicious coffees I have ever tasted. We always clamored around him to be the first to taste the coffee. He never gave us more than a teaspoon but it tasted so sweet and so heavenly. My parents, God fearing folks, worked hard to ensure that we went to school and were not lacking in basic necessities. They instilled in us core values like hard work and being truthful. I remember my father always said *'don't lie there crying, when you fall, it is ok to cry, but stand up, learn the lesson of why you fell and be a better person'*. We lived in a polygamous home.

Disaster stroke when one morning my mother dragged me and my three other siblings out of the house crying and telling us we were leaving. I could not have been more than 7 years old. My mother had bruises all over her face, her eyes were red and swollen and she was some-what limping. My two younger sisters must have been five and three and my brother just a baby being carried on one hand by mother as she gathered the rest of us with the other hand. I was so frightened and started screaming, I didn't want to go so I called out for my father but he was nowhere to be found. I felt lost, abandoned and helpless. I asked myself why my father was not there. Did he truly want us to leave? Why was my mother crying, was she in an accident and why was she leaving? My mother wouldn't answer my questions. The fact was, my parents were separating.

We lived with one relative or another under conditions sometimes that were so inhumane. I recall one of the relatives didn't have room for us but cleared one of the chicken barns for us to sleep in. The stench was unbearable. We preferred playing till late in the night rather than go into the barn and be bitten over and over by ticks. The relative had also given a piece of farmland to my mother. My mother built a thatched stick hut on it in which we lived in abject poverty. I later learned as I grew up that women couldn't own property let alone a piece of land. All the land she had earlier been farming on belonged to my father. I cried every morning when I saw the other children going to school. My mother would console me by saying *'You still have time to go to school'*. She later explained that the only reason I was in school was because I would follow my elder step siblings to school even though my right hand couldn't touch my left ear, which is how it was determined then whether a child was of age to attend school.

My step sister's teacher ended up letting me stay in the class to avoid me crying. Not being able to go to school was the end of my world. I was so miserable. My mother couldn't afford to send me to school. I could feel and see pain and anguish in her. She worked hard, slept very little and cried a lot when alone. It broke my heart. My fun memory of that era was Christmas day, the only day of the year my mother cooked rice in chunky pork fat pieces after saving pennies to afford that. I would run around the village with my friends holding the piece of pork fat in my palm, licking the pork oil trickling down my arm having turns with my friends. We had little but we shared, making sure one of them didn't grab my pork fat and dash into the bushes. It was also about survival of the fittest.

My elder step-brother and his wife adopted me and took me to continue school in Buea so I could also help look after their children. I was so happy, for there was hope for me to go back to school. I had completely lost hope of ever going back to school. I promised myself to make good use of this opportunity by working very hard and giving my mother and siblings better living conditions. So, I set out to be a very hard working *'good girl'* as they would later call me. It was important to me that everybody be happy with me. I was always the first to get out of bed, help to clean the house, wash and iron clothes, cook and care for my niece and nephews. It was hard on me. There were nights I spent crying but I never complained.

That day in October 1980, as I strode down from the stage in the graduation hall clinging to the precious piece of paper I had just received like it was a matter of life and death, the scene of me opening my eyes and seeing a beautiful angelic white lady sitting by my bed holding my hand and smiling into my eyes suddenly reappeared. It was not a vision, it happened. I was about 11 years old. I remember feeling sick and feverish at school. By the time I was rushed to hospital, I was unconscious. I was in coma for over a month. As I woke up the first thing I saw was this Lady in a white coat. I thought she was my guardian angel. She spoke in a kind, gentle musical voice **'do not worry, do not be afraid you are fine, all will be well'.** She wanted to know whether I was in pain, if I had any discomfort or was hungry etc. She looked so serene. Her attention was just overwhelming. I started crying, that was when she held me in her arms and started crying also.

For a longtime she was shaking, I was shaking and she wiped my tears and gave me a kiss on my forehead. My 'Mother' who had hardly left my bedside told me the Doctor Lady came to my bedside several times a day. She continued to do so for the period I spent in the hospital. I was so moved by such dedication, compassion and love. She explained to me why I was sick. A year prior to me getting into coma, I had fallen in the bathtub causing a crack in my right tibia. This later developed into the bone and a blood infection, which led to the coma. I just knew then that when I grew up I wanted to be like her. I would be a Doctor. She later transferred me to a more specialize hospital for surgery. I never saw her again. She just disappeared into thin air like Angels do. The hospital decided to amputate my leg. My parents, very upset by the decision decided to take me to Ibadan teaching hospital where my cousin was a Surgeon. Because of the Biafra war, he instead came home to do the surgery and saved my leg from amputation.

This illness had killed once more my hope for continuing school. I stayed home to heal. I was so miserable. My 'Father' who was a journalist had just been posted to start English language programs in the radio station in Douala which is in French speaking Cameroon. He took me along and enrolled me for one term in a French speaking secondary school (Lycée de Jeunes Filles, Douala). I couldn't speak a word of French. But it was such an exciting experience for me that I worked very hard and by the end of the term I had pass marks in most of the subjects. Both the Directress of the school and my 'father' were so impressed that I was enrolled in the school as a case study. I graduated seven years later with honors.

I have often asked myself why such a short encounter with the Lady Doctor would leave such an indelible mark on me. It was not until several years later while in medical school that I realized that God put her on my path so I could see, feel and touch my purpose. It was about touching and positively impacting people and that my path to fulfilling this was through the field of medicine. My childhood taught me that when all seems desperate, do not lose hope for God has a plan for you. Through the Yoruba proverb: *it takes a village to raise a child*. God's plan was accomplished. The village raised me out of poverty.

Achieving my purpose:

As a young medical doctor, I believed all I needed to do was to continue working very hard, giving the best of me to my patients, being loving, caring and compassionate. So I strived for excellence and perfection in my work.

It was government policy to post newly graduated medical doctors to under-privileged areas in Cameroon, which had very few or no doctors. My first posting was to Bamenda General Hospital. The most scaring and challenging experience I had there, concerned a 24-year-old woman with a ruptured ectopic pregnancy. On my first night duty, I was called in to perform surgery on her! I was scared. Not because I couldn't do the surgery but because I was pre-occupied about the way the nurses would judge me, I was afraid of failing. Most of all I wanted to perform a perfect surgery for my patient. I wanted to save her, she had bled a lot and I was worried about that. This would be the first time I had sole responsibility of the outcome of the surgery.

Even though I did this kind of surgery during training it was always under the responsibility of the chief surgeon. I felt the weight of that responsibility on me. What if something went wrong and I couldn't handle it? What if she died? Too many 'what ifs' clouded my vision. As I stood there scrubbing-in, it was as if all I knew about the subject had suddenly left my brain. My hands were trembling and I could feel little pebbles of perspiration on my forehead. I felt like running out of the room. All eyes were on me. So I took a deep breath, counted to ten and asked myself if this was the kind of perfect doctor I dreamed I would be. Naturally, I wouldn't tell the theater nurse that I was scared let alone ask for his help. Nor would I even dare ask that another colleague be called. I braced myself and started. The surgery went well because the theater nurse could see my plight as he later told me. He was very gentle in assisting me and sometimes even directing me if I let him. I was the Doctor, remember? I can do it! This experience was an eye opener to me. I was thankful to the theater nurse and to all those like him who have held the hands of so many like me lifting us up. To them I say Salute! You are my Heroes. I wondered then what I really meant by being a perfect doctor. But I didn't pay much attention to that question. I worked harder.

Being the first at work and the last to leave, I created between my patients and my team a friendly working environment of trust, confidence, selflessness, dedication and compassion. This dedication was not wasted on our patients as many came back being very grateful and thankful. My greatest fulfillment was seeing the joy in my patients when I encountered them in places such as the market, church or at social gatherings. They would come up to me saying 'Doctor, thank you again for all you did' holding and shaking my hand so hard. I was always very sad when one of my patients died. It was heart breaking when I had to encounter the family and explain what happened. There were a lot of unexpected challenges. Many patients died because they couldn't afford to buy the prescribed medications. Sometimes the hospital didn't have the technical platform to provide proper care to the patients. If that were the case they would need to be transferred to a referral hospital sometimes hundreds of kilometers away with poor access roads. Many of the patients arrived too late at our hospital for one reason or another: no money, lived very far from hospital, poor access roads etc. This was very frustrating and cast a shadow to my vision of perfection in the practice of medicine. I increasingly spent my money on my patients needing care.

A year after graduation I got married and started having children. Little did I know that these beautiful happenings in my life would add to the challenges of fulfilling my promise to being the perfect doctor. Besides having anxiety and sleepless nights in the hospital I had sleepless nights as a wife and mother. I had to make sure everything was perfect both at home and at work. A clean beautiful house, a happy husband with all his exquisite meals cooked only by me, healthy happy children. I promised myself I would give my children the dreamland childhood I never had. And so, they attended the best schools, well dressed, had best foods and toys, dropped and picked from school, sports events and birthday parties, and the whole family went to church every Sunday. In addition I had to cater for the needs of my mother and siblings (school, food, and lodging). They also were my responsibility. I soon realized that the financial implications of all these responsibilities were huge. I told myself it was not about me. It was foremost about the others, my patients, family and friends. I wanted to please at all cost, I even felt guilty when I would spend a few CFA francs on myself.

Despite all these responsibilities I believed it was in everyone's interest for me to specialize. That would help me move up the ladder in my profession and be able to give specialized care to my patients. And definitely also earn more money. My monthly salary then was about 400 US dollar and as a specialist I would earn about 700 US dollar monthly. My undergraduate thesis was on river blindness and I had felt that there was a great need to improve eye health in Cameroon. There were then very few ophthalmologists in Cameroon and all located in the two major cities. I sought and was awarded a World Health Organization (WHO) Scholarship to study ophthalmology in Glasgow, Great Britain. I was elated but sad about leaving my young family behind especially my 18 month old baby. I was convinced of the necessity to go. Nothing would stop me. Not even the fact that I discovered a week before departure that I was a few weeks pregnant.

I arrived Glasgow in the fall. It was so cold. I had never experienced such cold in my life. So cold that I would dress like it was winter already. This drew surprised glances and camouflaged smiles from passers on the street and campus. I didn't care. I had to do what I had to do. I felt so lonely, my husband who had accompanied me had returned home. I was alone in a foreign country, cold and suffering from morning sickness. There were mornings I just laid curled up in my bed so sick and exhausted asking myself what I was doing here. Worst of all I didn't understand a word of what people said to me! Mind you they spoke English but it sounded so foreign. The accent was so different. It took me a whole school term to understand the professors. It was a nightmare for me meeting the patients because of the language barrier. However, I worked hard spending very long hours in the library, discussing with senior students who were sympathetic to me. I worked even harder. I was so distraught, so unhappy and just wanted to go back home. One Sunday morning I got up determined to go to church. The first church I saw was a Presbyterian church. Mind you I am catholic but that didn't matter. To me I would pray to the same God. I needed so badly to pray, to have a conversation with God. Why was he making things so difficult for me? I wanted to go home but that would mean failure. I was ashamed of what my colleagues, friends and even family would say, they would laugh at me. I would rather die than go through such shame. I repeatedly prayed: **God please help me!** And over time God heard my prayer. The members of this church became God's saving grace to me. This congregation became the social and spiritual support system that helped me throughout my stay. The church members and pastor would visit me often. One family even adopted me as their 'daughter'. Armed with this support, I worked even harder. I remember 9 months pregnant, as I was dragging my long tummy into the eye clinic one of my supervisors was so shocked to see me that she screamed in front of all the patients ***"Grace, what are you doing here, go back to your hostel and don't come back until you have had that baby"***. I just stood there frozen wondering what just happened here. Was she angry? Or mad at me or ashamed of me? She was smiling though, she probably just wanted me to rest. But I felt frustrated and ashamed. I had my son a few days later by caesarian section and a week later had to write exams. I didn't have a babysitter. I had not looked for one because of scary stories going around. For example, one student had left her baby in the care of a family and only visited during the weekends. After a year the family wanted to keep the baby and wouldn't let the mother visit claiming she was absent too often. It so happened the wife of a fellow student in my hostel was a stay at home mum. She offered to help as a temporarily solution.

Every morning I would wrap my son warmly, put him in his Moses' basket and slide the basket into the lady's corridor. She was always there to pick him up and care for him the whole day until 9 pm when I got back. My son and I had very tough nights. He insisted on breast feeding the whole night. I needed to study and sleep. He would cry and I would cry. We spent every night between crying, catching few moments of sleep and studying. I was exhausted and at the brink of mental breakdown. There were moments I felt like this was not my baby. If he loves me why would he not understand that I needed to rest, study and pass these exams for both our sakes. These were crazy thoughts going through my mind!!! At the end of three months I took the baby home before I lost my mind. There was a better support system back home. My mother and younger sister were already helping to take care of my baby I left. The heart-breaking part here was that when I arrived at the airport in Yaoundé, my sister said to my 2-year-old daughter ***'see mama, go to mama'***. My daughter refused to come to me clinging to my sister crying and calling her mama! This was shocking, I never anticipated that my child would forget me. And it stroke me like lighting! During my one month stay I had to do everything to win her back. The mother guilt in me was just overwhelming. I over compensated in every aspect. Leaving my children was too high a price to pay. Every great achievement comes with a high price tag.

I returned to Glasgow to finish that first part of my training during which I realized curative ophthalmology was not what I needed to better serve my patients back home. I believed there was a need for more prevention than treating each case that came to the hospital. So I enrolled in the International Centre for eye health (ICEH) in London where the courses were more public health oriented. But before starting, I went home and came back with my children in addition to one of my nieces. The aim being my niece would further her education in hair dressing and cosmetics. We arrived London in the heart of winter. I recall one day they locked themselves out of the house and spent the day out in the snow in front of the door. Usually I would call my niece several times a day to find out how they were doing. That day she wouldn't pick my calls. I was so afraid. I couldn't imagine what had happened. Had the house burnt down? Were they Ok? By 4pm, I had to leave class and rush back home. Just to find them in a neighbor's house who after hours of seeing them standing in the snow had called them in and given some milk to my screaming 10-month-old son. This was yet another incident that made me wonder why I had to go through all this.

At the end of my training, one of my psychology professors made the following appraisal of me *"Dr Fobi, you are hardworking, conscientious, you know what you want and are committed to achieving it at all cost. You want perfection in everything you do. Remember it is difficult to reach perfection. You cannot be a perfect professional, a perfect mother and a perfect wife. You are a human being and all humans have limitations. Learn to recognize your limitations. You would be a better person"*. I realized how shockingly correct he was. This was the rude-awakening I much needed. I looked back at my family, social and professional life. To achieve the perfection which I sought, I drove everyone around me to the limits of their own abilities, to the point I created so many enemies around me. Especially my colleagues who were purely clinic based ophthalmologists and considered the public health ophthalmology degree I had to be below them. This was still a new, poorly understood field for many.

One of them even went as far as accusing a student of plagiarism whose thesis I supervised. We had included in the thesis pictures of hypertensive retinopathy which we took. The colleague did not believe I had the appropriate equipment in my research team, let alone the ability to take such high-resolution pictures of the fundus. The student and I were exonerated and the colleague received a blame from the disciplinary council. To me the driving force was to put a smile on my patient's faces, make my family and friends happy and proud of me. For instance, within a short time of returning home, I had started so many initiatives to improve eye care in Cameroon.

Even though I worked in a government hospital I convinced a Non-Governmental Developmental Organization (NGDO) to collaborate with the ophthalmology unit in providing consumables for cataract surgery in this hospital. The cost of cataract surgery went from 350 000 francs CFA to about 25 000 francs CFA. This was a major win for our patients. I also started with other foreign NGDO, missions to Yaoundé to offer free eye consultations, free eye glasses, and free surgery. Most importantly I started the development of the program document for national eye care in collaboration with several NGDOs and colleagues. I worked with other colleagues to revamp the Cameroon Association for Ophthalmologists etc. I was also the Lead ophthalmologist in a multidisciplinary research team on river blindness funded by the World Health Organization. Besides these, I did my daily diligence of attending to patients in the Eye Unit and attended short courses and numerous conferences. I was so busy, tired and exhausted. I later joined the World Health Organization (WHO) and worked in a top management position for the control of River Blindness in 31 countries in Africa.

Lessons:

I don't think I set out knowing the path that would lead me to becoming a medical Doctor. Let alone a perfect one! The important thing for me was to have recognized what I wanted to become. My whole being then worked like an auto-pilot plane honed to reaching that target. It is all about resilience and creating walls into doors to achieve your purpose and not being afraid to venture into new professional pathways best suited to your ambitions. I revisited the conversation with my psychology professor several times and the greatest lesson I learned was ***becoming a better me***: a better professional, a better mother and a better wife. Life is not about being the best. It is about becoming better every day doing ordinary things in life with passion, commitment and stamina knowing that God walks every step with you.

I became more conscious of myself, my body and mind creating space for me in my life. It is important to have your secret space/garden. For me it is a physical flower garden. I made time to work in my garden, or just sit there sipping my first cup of coffee listening to birds and watching the early morning sun rise. It brings me so much tranquility, joy and allows me to organize my thoughts. Nature is a pure example of organization. Even when we think there is chaos, there is a method to it. And don't let anybody tell you that you don't deserve to be happy. Remember you can only take care of others if you are physically and mentally healthy. Make your health your number one priority.

It is ok to fail. The important thing is to learn from failure, become better and try again. Beverly Sills says **'There are no shortcuts to any place worth going'**. The price tag might be high but it is worth paying it.

Training to the highest level of your profession gives you the needed confidence and humility to allow you to see and accept your limitations. There is an African proverb that says '**It takes two hands to tie a bundle**' in this case the use of several brains gives the best care plan to your patient. The greatest example about recognizing limitations is given to me by my daughter. Have you ever been driving and your whole body is telling you stop and rest but your brain keeps saying you are just 10 minutes away. At that point stop.

Creating a strong team, delegating responsibilities and sharing credit with co-workers makes a win-win situation for everyone.

Write your obituary while alive! Publications are a good way to let others know about your work. Mentorship of younger colleagues, young people especially empowering the girl child ensures lasting legacy. You can only improve the world from where you are standing.

Know when to exit. Prepare yourself mentally, physically and financially for your retirement. Retirement is the time when you do what you want, where you want, when you want and with whom you want.

I have learned to put God at the forefront of all I do. *'For I know the plans I have for you', declares the Lord, 'plans to prosper you and not to harm you, plans to give you hope and a future' Jeremiah 29:11* God's plan for me has always unfolded itself in a way that left me wondering why I ever worried. God is always with me! I have learned to be thankful, grateful and count my blessings every day. My daughter always says *'put life on a scale, you will see it always tilts positively. The negative happenings highlight the power of God.'*

DEDICATION

To my 'MOTHERS', Mama Monica Nchang and Mami Sally Neba-Fabs, the silent and constant forces behind who I am. I **AM** because you **WERE** and I **AM** because you **ARE**. You taught me the true meaning of 'MOTHER'

Dr. Grace A. Neba Fobi

Grace Fobi is a retired Public Health Ophthalmologist with over 10 years of experience in the management of regional and national programs for the *Control & Elimination of River Blindness* and other *Neglected Tropical Diseases* in Africa.

A big part of her career was focused on River blindness also known as *Onchocerciasis,* a disease whose consequences include irreversible blindness, community emigration and aggravation of poverty. About 120 million people in 31 countries in Africa are at risk. The disease is also found in some countries in Latin America and in Yemen.

Grace Fobi has been privileged to be part of a formidable team at the African Program for onchocerciasis Control (APOC), which worked relentlessly within an unprecedented partnership of Donors, NGDOs, African Governments and affected communities to create sustainable distribution systems to reach people at risk of the disease. These at-risk communities tend to have no access to doctors, hospitals, or functional health systems. With the medicine *Mectizan (Ivermectine)*, freely donated by *Merck & Co.* through its *Mectizan Donation Program (MDP),* Dr. Fobi and her team were able to reach these communities. Building on the successes of prior programs, *APOC'*s work has brought the disease down to a point where today, its elimination can be considered in many countries in Africa. Proud to have contributed her tiny footprint to the giant walk of mankind in the fight against River blindness, Grace Fobi now spends her time between her passions of gardening, travelling and her God given job of grandma.

Dr. Luegenia Ndi
Board Certified Internal Medicine

BALANCING THE TIPPING SCALES

The school bell rang and I leaped to my feet in exhilaration. It was the last day of summer school and I was already tired of the flat drone of my teacher's voice. It wasn't just that he was boring; I missed my friends terribly and couldn't wait to return to the bustling halls of our boarding school where the fun of mischief almost outweighed the passion for A grades. I skipped along home, lost in silent happy thoughts, expertly hopping the large puddles that littered my path; evidence of the heavy rains that pounded the city this morning. It was July and we expected such weather in this part of the world, just as we expected drivers to cautiously dodge the crate sized potholes that besieged the roads for the sake of innocent pedestrians. Well, someone didn't get the memo; I thought, as one rudely left me a brown muddy mess as he sped by. Urrggghh! Luckily, my grandmother's house was only a few more blocks away.

I rushed in with just one thought in mind – shower. Barely stopping to say hi to the visitor sitting at the table, I breezed by. But wait, it looked like him. Oh gosh, it was him of the puppy brown eyes, side gap tooth and a lazy smile. He was Lennon; my summer crush who had barely spoken to me all this while. And here he was; today of all days when I was the complete picture of imperfection. Why hadn't he stopped by this morning when I was a walking ad for *SoftSheen Carson*, sporting waves still fresh in shiny perfection? Or maybe yesterday when everyone complimented my looks. Why today? Why now? Life was so unfair!

My palms sweated, the loud pounding of my chest echoed to my own ears and still he continued to smile. He was here to see my cousin, he explained when I inquired. Wait, why was I still standing here making small talk in my mud-trodden self? I quickly excused myself and reappeared sometime later, decked in a beautiful summer dress. I may have scattered other outfits on my bed as I scrambled to find the perfect look, but hey, he doesn't have to know that!

Our conversation flowed easily. Female boarder meets male boarder and here comes endless tales of boarding school drama. Our summer experiences were different yet similar; we even had common friends. On and on we went, as the hours went by without notice. Did he come again to visit my cousin? It was obvious even to the untrained eye that we had a very strong connection which neither one of us could explain. As we went back to our respective schools a few weeks later, we could hardly wait for the next holidays when we would meet again.

****

I grew up with my grandmother, who was known in the community as a no-nonsense woman. As a single mother, she worked tirelessly to make sure her children and grandchildren had the best in life. Grandma was a feminist, even if we did not know it at the time. She instilled in us the importance of chasing our dreams: of self-worth and personal validation. Grandma always reminded me I was my own person and did not need a man to validate me. A product of a society heavily steeped in patriarchy, grandma's ideology was a doctrine of passive resistance. But she would also teach me other values of womanhood, greatly endeared in our African society: respect, good housekeeping, pleasantness and hard work.

Communications with my mother were present, but infrequent. We had no landline telephone and cell phones were still a luxury of the future. Every chance to talk to her was a cherished opportunity I did not take for granted, even if it required me making a mile-long walk to a family friend's house to make use of the telephone. Our conversations were never long enough; there was no calling card long enough to convey all the things I wanted to tell my mother. So, I waited in listless anticipation for the day when I would finally join her in the US and tell her all the things I was bursting to say. I was a flighty one when it came to career aspirations. Today I wanted to become a doctor, tomorrow it was an engineer, and the next day a lawyer. Ask me what all these professions entailed, and I probably couldn't tell you. However, it appeared I had nurtured the desire for helping the sick with simple task as changing my grandmother's bandages from a festering wound. My grandmother and mother concurred; these were all noble choices, but doctor was the noblest of them all. And just like that I made the decision; I would become a doctor. That came with the increased academic pressure for excellent grades, but it wasn't an impossible feat to achieve. A little less goofing around, an extra hour or two of study each day and I was thriving as any young medical hopeful.

Socially, perhaps not so well. Another holiday rolled by and my mother thought spending the holidays with a family friend in another city would be a welcome change for me. They had a house phone so I could talk to mom often. Finally! It was also the first time I would live in a two-parent household. I was unprepared for the comforting monotony of both parents leaving home early every morning and family suppers when the family gathered as one to a recap of each other's day. And I was especially unprepared for the calm confidence of children firmly secure in the unquestionable love and daily presence of both parents. Often, I would question myself and what it was about me that made it so easy for my father to walk and stay out of my life with little thought or reason. I must have done something wrong; but for the life of me, I couldn't tell what it was. Many a day too, I would shun the spicy delight of food and lose myself behind the house to the river of my tears in sorrow for all I was missing out of in terms of family life. But thank heavens for good 'ole Lennon. He was the only friend I would share my worries with and the only one who's understanding, calm but sometimes stern counsel could make me grudgingly smile or snap back to reality when I wanted to wallow in self-pity for too long.

*****

For as long as I could remember, I had always been proud of my unique heritage and village of strong independent women who helped raise me. I still was; but was now learning that feminine strength, independence and family were not mutually exclusive. The matriarch of my present home epitomized the perfect blend of family and career. She was a Judge, renowned for her sass and feared for her courtroom iron-fist. But at home, she was just "dear" to her besotted husband and "mummy" to the kids she so shamelessly doted on. I admired that and I wanted that in my future. And so, I shelved that thought in the recesses of my heart, hoping life would give me a chance to revisit that one day.

The years went on, uneventful for the mostly. High school came and went; the flurry of pictures on graduation day, cherished memories I would carry on of the friends who had been an integral part of my life for many years.

*****

It was time to leave the comforting familiarity of my grandmother's Cameroonian nest to the unknown grandeur of my mother's American home. It was a power tussle from the first day- she was a novice wielding parental authority; and I was a hormonal teenager trying to find my own person and make meaning of this thing called life.

By this time, Lennon and I had mutually agreed to give chance to a long-distance relationship and like any smart

African child; I tried to keep that information away from the prying ears. But like any inquisitive African parent, mom found in no time, and boy was she livid! I was in no place to be thinking of a relationship, I was not ready for one, why was I trying to ruin my future, I would destroy my life, I had to stop that relationship immediately…On and on mom went; her voice the high octave it always took when she was furious. Well, what else could I do? I continued to see him. Or did you think it was that easy to sway a teenage girl hopelessly in love? But I also understood where mom was coming from; she just did not want me to be another statistic of broken dreams like she and grandma were. So within me, I vowed not to fall off the high pedestal she had placed me on.

A few years later, Lennon joined me in the United States, and we knew the road ahead of us was paved with many challenges. We were young and many naysayers scoffed at our dreams of making it. For one, money was tight. Extremely tight. Lennon was on a student visa and had to cough up onwards three times what a domestic student paid in tuition every semester to stay in lawful legal status. So, first thing we did was to each get a nurses' aid license so we could work. Work we did. In between classes, sixteen-hour shifts became a regular occurrence as we scrambled to pick up every open shift allowed. Had federal labor laws not barred it, we probably would have been willing to pull in a 24—hour shift once or twice. When I wasn't lifting up residents at the nursing home, I was braiding hair to secure another $50 for our ever-mounting heap of bills. But amidst all the craziness, we never for once lost sight of our personal goals.

I completed my prerequisites and was accepted to nursing school at Texas Tech University Health Sciences Center. One year into the nursing program, I qualified to sit in for the License Practical Nursing board exam. I quickly grabbed the opportunity and earned my LPN license. Being an LPN meant more money; at least now I would get more than $ 600 after breaking my back for two weeks. What relief!

School and work took up a good portion of our time, but we still made time for our budding little family. I breezed through nursing school and landed my first job as a Registered Nurse before anyone could say when. My exit was Lennon's entry; so thoroughly planned and well-calculated was our master plan which was unfolding with no hiccups. While he was in school, I was taking prerequisites for medical school, preparing for the MCAT (Medical college entrance test.).

*****

Few months after I took the exam, my MCAT results came in and I was floored- I had done poorly. It would be my first experience at academic failure and the onslaught of tears was uncontrollable. Maybe I wasn't cut out to be a doctor, I often wondered aloud to the chastisement of Lennon. Under his constant encouragement and relentless insistence, I fearfully registered for the MCAT again. This would be the last time I took this exam; if I didn't make it this time, it was a wrap; I grudgingly thought. We had two ever hungry little mouths to feed now and we did not have money to keep throwing about.

And so, began several months of intense study as I shielded myself in quiet seclusion. It was a continuous rigid cycle of work, home, and study that even my little baby must have noticed, but had no words to question. My scores this time around were a minute improvement from the former. I was devastated and swore that was the end of my dreams of becoming a doctor. Nursing was good enough; thank you very much. After all didn't doctors and nurses both wear scrubs and work under the same settings to help mankind? I was done! But here comes Lennon with his convincing voice of reason... And so I began studying for the MCAT. Again! Until one day I received a call out of nowhere "Good afternoon, this is Lindsey at the Oklahoma State University admission office; I am calling to offer you an admission into our upcoming medical school class." Well surprise, surprise! I screamed so loud all the nurses came rushing in thinking my patient was coding (cardiopulmonary arrest). It was a celebratory mood all around as everybody seemed excited for me; even the ones who had doubted my resolve.

Well, the excitement was short-lived and tampered by some of the serious life-changing decisions we had to make as a family. For one, my husband had an excellent job; were we going to throw away that financial security? Second, we were new homeowners; it would have been financially crippling to put our house on the market at that time with the country going through a recession. And what about the children? How were we going to be able to manage childcare with tight schedules and limited income? In the end, we decided for a short while, the children will be raised by their grandparents in Cameroon, keep the house, temporarily move me to Oklahoma and pursue our individual career dreams.

*****

Having the children live in another continent was by far the hardest decision I had to make. I cried, sniffed, and cried some more as I questioned whether medical school was worth the loss of time with them. Even though the separation would only be for a few years, it was still heart-wrenching. They were in good trustworthy hands but the mother in me could not stop worrying if they would be ok, and if they would handle the separation well. Gosh, I missed my babies. I arrived Oklahoma a broken wreck just before the tedious journey of medical school began. Medical school was all what I'd heard it to be; and more. It was laborious; certainly, no ride in the park for the faint of heart. It was many hours of diligent study, managing an insane workload while completing rotations and preparing for career decisive STEP exams. Your time was no longer your own and you learned another side of death: the death of the freedom you once had; of the pleasure of the things you once enjoyed and perhaps, to some, of the relationships you once held.

I would battle all these as a new medical student, while still trying to keep in touch with my family every single day. Every chance I got; I made the 18 plus hour flight to Cameroon to behold the sweet innocence of my babies. I had a respite two years into medical school when my mother-in-law was granted permanent residency in the US and relocated with the children to Lubbock. I'd take that 7hour drive to Lubbock over an 18-hour flight across multiple international lines, any day, any time.

Wearing the hats of wife, mom, student, sometimes-frequent-flyer and sometimes-roadrunner was no picnic. But then, I was a product of tough stock; made for stuff like this. I was still proudly graduated in the top 20% of my medical school class and was inducted into the Sigma Sigma Phi Osteopathic Honor Society.

*****

Match day came and I successfully matched to my #1 choice of residency. I could finally go back to Lubbock to be reunited with my family! Although I was reunited with my family, residency was tough. The excitement of being at home and sleeping once again daily in the comforting arms of my Lennon and bam, your girl was knocked up, again. I had to learn to survive on 3 to 4 hour sleep a day, while battling pregnancy. I had survived medical school alone with my sanity intact and this would not be different not especially now with plenty of support. Hence, with my ever-supportive friends and family by my side, we welcomed our daughter and I successfully moved on from being called Resident Doctor to Attending Physician. Life could not get better

*****

Today, my grandmother and mother are quick to tell every ear that cares to listen (and a few who couldn't be bothered) how proud they are of me and the woman I have become. And just as quickly, I am quick to remind them that this wasn't all me. This is the work of my ever-supportive family who refused to let me limit myself. Where would I be today if grandma hadn't reiterated to me the importance of chasing one's dreams from such an early age? Where would I be if mom hadn't set me on so high a pedestal that I knew failure wasn't an option? Where would I be if my husband, Lennon, hadn't relentlessly pushed me to pick up the reins of disappointment and take the MCAT one more time? Where would I be if my mother-in-law hadn't selflessly opted to take care of the children so I could go chase my dreams?

I want you to know that dreams are meant to be held onto even when the path seems daunting. If you are fortunate to have the support of family and friends like I did, then you are blessed. However, when others do not believe in you or doubt the choices you make, always believe in yourself and find that inner strength to keep forging ahead and staying grounded. For me, my Christian values and heritage provided the buffer I needed to handle life's curveballs. I have colleagues who after achieving extreme success are today regretting that they are not married or do not have children. Some may have had the opportunity while pursuing their careers but because of family pressure of wanting to be the perfect child or just shear stress of not wanting to jungle relationships with school, missed out on a beautiful journey.

Others unfortunately missed out through no fault of theirs; life is funny like that.

I would be the first to agree that marriage is not a bed of roses and juggling career and family in a highly charged society is anything but easy. But my dream is to encourage another couple that it is doable as long as both partners remain committed to each other. If there is anything to take away of my story, it is the fact that commitment is the key to the success of any relationship. My relationship with Lennon continued and thrived because we were both committed to making it work. We were kids when we met, and pretty much kids when we got married. We didn't know much about life or how to be married, but we shared a strong commitment to each other and therefore made our marriage work. We respected each other's interests and allowed each other follow their dreams. Most importantly, we always recognized that being together was worth working through our issues.

*****

When I look back at my life, I can see that I have been one lucky lady. The life of a physician can be very chaotic but even a weeklong bedlam in the hospital could never make me regret this wonderful, fulfilling and sometimes stressful career I pursued. Providing a strong and stable home for my children while still being an educated woman, a role model and a productive member of society has been a dream. Even though I go home to toy-littered bedrooms and three very chatty children with endless demands from their mummy, I know my life has come full circle. Life is great now. I am still married to my childhood crush whom I met all those years ago in all my muddy elegance in grandma's living room.

Dr. Luegenia Ndi

Dr. Luegenia Ndi is a Board Certified Internal Medicine physician at Covenant Medical Center in Lubbock Texas. Born and raised in Southern Cameroons, Dr. Ndi completed her secondary education at the prestigious Saker Baptist College. She later earned her Bachelor's Degree in Nursing from Texas Tech University Health Sciences Center in 2006. Dr. Ndi went on to work as a Registered Nurse for several years before pursuing a career in Medicine. In 2015, she obtained her medical degree with honors at the Oklahoma State University Center for Health Sciences. Dr. Ndi completed her Internal Medicine residency at Texas Tech University Health Sciences Center in Lubbock, Texas. She has been in clinical practice since 2006 and in her spare time, Dr. Ndi enjoys community building activities, dancing, cooking and spending quality time with family and friends. She is married to Lennon and together are raising 3 children.